Sermon Science

Sermon Science

*How the Laws of Learning
Can Increase Sermon Impact
and Change Lives*

GREGORY J. CIZEK

WIPF & STOCK · Eugene, Oregon

SERMON SCIENCE
How the Laws of Learning Can Increase Sermon Impact and Change Lives

Copyright © 2025 Gregory J. Cizek. All rights reserved. Except for brief quotations in critical publications or reviews, no part of this book may be reproduced in any manner without prior written permission from the publisher. Write: Permissions, Wipf and Stock Publishers, 199 W. 8th Ave., Suite 3, Eugene, OR 97401.

Wipf & Stock
An Imprint of Wipf and Stock Publishers
199 W. 8th Ave., Suite 3
Eugene, OR 97401

www.wipfandstock.com

PAPERBACK ISBN: 979-8-3852-4213-9
HARDCOVER ISBN: 979-8-3852-4214-6
EBOOK ISBN: 979-8-3852-4215-3

New Living Translation (NLT)
Unless otherwise indicated, all Scripture quotations are taken from the Holy Bible, New Living Translation, copyright © 1996, 2004, 2015 by Tyndale House Foundation. Used by permission of Tyndale House Publishers, Carol Stream, Illinois 60188. All rights reserved.

New International Version (NIV)
Scripture quotations marked NIV are taken from the Holy Bible, New International Version®, NIV®. Copyright © 1973, 1978, 1984, 2011 by Biblica, Inc.™ Used by permission of Zondervan. All rights reserved worldwide. www.zondervan.com The "NIV" and "New International Version" are trademarks registered in the United States Patent and Trademark Office by Biblica, Inc.™

English Standard Version (ESV)
Scripture quotations marked ESV are from The Holy Bible, English Standard Version®, © 2001 by Crossway, a publishing ministry of Good News Publishers. Used by permission. All rights reserved.

Image Credits
Figure 2-4 (Application Grid) originally published by 9Marks.org Used with permission of 9Marks Ministries, 525 A Street NE, Washington, DC 20002.
Figure 2-1: Seneca, after Peter Paul Rubens, Public domain, via Wikimedia Commons
Figure 2-2: Created by Buz11 and used by permission, CC BY-SA 4.0
Figure 2-5: My Wife and My Mother-in-Law, W. E. Hill (1915), public domain, via Wikipedia Commons
Figure 5-9: (eyes) I, KnowItSome, Creative Commons-Share Alike 3.0 Unported; (cake) jan Alonola, Creative Commons Attribution-Share Alike 4.0 International; (ambulance) Kaive26 Creative Commons-Share Alike 3.0 Unported
Figure 5-10: DieselFordMondeo, CC BY-SA 4.0
Figure 5-11: Jetsons Flying Car image, Creative Commons CC BY-SA
Figure 5-12: Shark fin, uryadnikov, www.Pond5.com
Figure 5-13: Portrait of William Wilberforce by Karl Anton Hickel (1794), public domain, via Wikimedia Commons
Figure 5-14: Image of St. Drogo, beeldhouwer, CC BY-SA 4.0
Figure 6-6: iClicker image courtesy of Macmillan Publishing, New York, NY
Back Cover: Looking through microscope, Creative Fabrica, Amsterdam

To my son, Stephen.

Contents

Preface xi

Chapter 1 – *Why Better Sermons?* | 1
   Sermons as Teaching and Learning Events | 3
   R-E-S-P-E-C-T | 4
   Achievable Goals | 7
   So Buckle Up | 9
   The Journey Ahead | 12
   Conclusions | 14

Chapter 2 – *Are You Ready?* | 15
   Turning Aptitude into Skill | 17
   Aspects of Preparation | 19
      Nevermind "Thyself" | 19
      What's the Point? | 22
      Getting to the Point | 25
      Linking to the Point | 30
      A Framework for Learning, Recall, and Application | 31
      Ensuring the Point is the Point | 37
   Conclusions | 41

Chapter 3 – *The Lectern and the Pulpit* | 43
   A Sermon Is Not a Lecture | 44
   Reading and Retelling | 45
   Philology: Whatever *That* Is! | 47
   Making Meaning Accessible | 50
   Respecting Persons . . . and Their Time | 56
      Reading | 57

Contents

  Repeating | 59
  Replaying | 60
 Conclusions | 62

Chapter 4 – *No Laughing Matter* | 64
 The Context of Humor | 64
 Three Perils of Humor | 66
  I Don't Get It | 66
  Disembodied Humor | 68
  Humor that Hurts | 68
 Humor that Helps | 70
 Conclusions | 77

Chapter 5 – *Vehicles* | 78
 The Contemporary Context | 79
 Slide Deck Presentations | 83
  Density | 84
  Piloting | 88
  Parsimony | 89
  Reading | 94
  Animation | 95
  An Addendum on Parsimony | 98
 Images | 99
 Stories | 105
 Examples | 108
 Non-Examples | 110
 An Emerging Caution | 115
 Conclusions | 116

Chapter 6 – *Testing: 1, 2, 3* | 117
 The Imperative for Information | 118
 Are You Saying to Give Tests in Church? | 118
 Two Benefits of Assessment in the Context of Sermons | 120
 Information about the Preaching | 120
  Formative Assessment | 120
  Feedback | 122
  Characteristics of Effective Feedback | 123
  The Role of Feedback | 125

Contents

    Feedback and Power | 126
    Potential Sources of Information | 128
        Dialogic Preaching | 129
        Self-Recording | 130
        Surveys | 130
        Preaching Circles | 135
    Summary | 136
Information about the Learning | 137
    Testing Reprised | 138
        How the Testing Effect Works | 140
        What Testing Might Look Like | 141
            Exit Tickets | 141
            Focus Groups | 144
            Surveys | 145
Conclusions | 146

CHAPTER 7 – *The Critical Friend* | 148
    What Is a Critical Friend? | 148
    The Critical Friend Environment and Process | 153
        Identifying Potential Candidates for a Critical Friend | 153
        Selection of a Critical Friend and Setting Expectations | 155
        Becoming Familiar with the Preaching Context | 155
        The Pre-Meeting | 156
        The Sermon Observation | 159
        Critical Analysis and Reflection | 162
        The Post-Meeting | 164
    Conclusion | 168

CHAPTER 8 – *Dear Pastor* | 168

About the Author | 175

Bibliography | 177

Preface

I AM NOT A pastor. I am not an expert on sermons.

I do, however, have fairly deep expertise in how people learn. My own doctoral work included preparation in an academic field called *instructional design*—the science of how teaching can best be organized to maximize impact on learning.

Despite clear differences, sermons are not unlike teaching, and I have been a teacher for thousands of students. My students have ranged from second graders at a small Christian school in northern Michigan to doctoral students at a large public university. In my academic life, I've also given over 200 professional presentations at scholarly conferences in my field.

An equally important qualification is that I have also been privileged to hear more than a thousand sermons over the course of my life so far; I hope to hear many more. I think I have benefitted enormously in my own spiritual growth from the sermons I've heard, and I am grateful to the many pastors who have sacrificed their time to foster that growth for me and others.

My purpose in writing this book is to make a connection between what we have learned about organizing effective teaching and what I have experienced listening to preaching. Much of what we know about how people learn can be applied to developing and delivering sermons. Those connections are dynamic, as the ways in which people learn in contemporary society are rapidly evolving, just as the incorporation of technology continues to change the face of sermons in many ways.

This is not a "how to" book. Readers won't find lists of "tips and tricks" for better preaching. Rather, I relate practical principles derived from what learning scientists have discovered help people learn to the context of organizing and delivering sermons. To illustrate their utility, I'll present those principles not as abstract, academic theories, but in situations that show

how they might be implemented. Although every situation is different, I've endeavored to describe the principles in such a way that readers will be able to easily adapt them to the many, diverse contexts in which creating and delivering sermons occurs.

If I were to distill the ideas covered in this entire book into two key points, it would be these:

1) It will be beneficial to reconceptualize sermon listeners as learners; and

2) Stimulating learning—that is, changes in thoughts, behaviors, and actions as a result of what has been preached—should be a primary concern. Toward that end, it is worthwhile considering what research in the field of instructional design has discovered about learning.

To elaborate on the first point just mentioned, I'll ask readers to consider reconceptualizing listeners as *learners*. Howard Hendricks hinted at this point in his book covering seven techniques he deemed necessary for conveying Biblical messages. Each chapter covered what he called a "law." The first letters of the titles for each chapter (The Laws of the *T*eacher, *E*ducation, *A*ctivity, *C*ommunication, the *H*eart, *E*ncouragement, and *R*eadiness) are an anagram that spell out the word *teacher*.[1]

The goal of any teaching is surely that learning follows. I suppose it is a minimal expectation that congregants hear and maybe even enjoy or appreciate a sermon. But that is not enough. As I will argue in this book, I believe a more helpful orientation is one that fosters active engagement with the sermon, that stimulates lasting recall and application of the intended content of a sermon, and that results in changed hearts, perspectives, actions. In short, that learning happens.

In various ways, the eight chapters in this book address the second point. In the following chapters, I address various aspects of preparing and delivering sermons through the lens of the science of instructional design. Not really a unique field in itself, *Sermon Science* is the application of evidence-based principles of teaching that can help listeners learn, retain, and be able to apply what they have heard in a sermon.

The first chapter, "Why Better Sermons?" provides the foundation for this relationship between principles of learning and sermons. Chapter 2 covers several precursors to creating a sermon, such as the importance of considering listeners' characteristics and what principles of instructional

---

1. Howard Hendricks, *Teaching to Change Lives*, 2003, p. 14.

Preface

design can tell us about how to organize a sermon. Chapter 3 draws parallels and distinctions between a sermon and a lecture, and it provides cautions so that the former doesn't turn into the latter. The topic of how to effectively use humor in a sermon is the topic of Chapter 4. Analogies, examples, narratives and other vehicles for conveying the main concepts in a sermon—whether involving traditional or contemporary technologies—and how those methods can aid listeners remember and apply what they learned in a sermon is the topic of Chapter 5. The topic of testing likely arouses anxious feelings in many readers, but testing is a well-documented key to learning. Although essentially non-existent in the contemporary practice of preaching, Chapter 6 chapter asks, "Why not?", and provides strategies for gathering self-assessment feedback that can be used to inform sermon organization and delivery, and information gathering strategies for incorporating learning checks as part of the sermon plan. Following on the focus of Chapter 6, an in-depth variation of gathering information for planning and delivering a sermon is a concept I've called the "Critical Friend" which is the topic of Chapter 7. The concept is defined, and the desirability of and process for including a Critical Friend in sermon preparation and delivery are provided. The concluding chapter, Chapter 8, circles back to what is, in essence, the primary aspiration of this book: to encourage those who prepare and deliver sermons.[2]

Now, a confession: Any helpful experiences, expertise, and insights that are represented in this book are simply passed along by me from the teaching, examples, and wisdom I've received from others. I first learned something about instructional design from a masterful mentor, Professor Stephen Yelon of Michigan State University. Steve has not only been a prolific contributor to what I've learned, but also to the fields of instructional design, teaching, and educational psychology over his four decades of research on teaching and learning.[3] I am also grateful for the candid comments on my teaching provided by the thousands of students over the years who completed instructional evaluation surveys in my courses. That honest input has helped me identify teaching behaviors and activities that have either helped or hindered my students' learning, allowing me to continually refine my own teaching practices.

2. Readers interested in following up on the topics covered in this book may wish to view the companion website, www.SermonScience.com

3. Among his influential contributions are Davis, Alexander, and Yelon, *Learning Systems Design*, Yelon and Weinstein, *A Teacher's World*, Yelon and Berge, "The Secret of Instructional Design," and Yelon, *Powerful Principles of Instruction*.

Preface

At least two spiritual mentors have also played a significant role in helping me reflect on my own teaching, on the connections between teaching and sermons, and have provided wise spiritual guidance. I am grateful to James Christians and Jim Huegerich for being my teachers, mentors, and friends. I also appreciate the insights of Professor Gerald McDermott (Distinguished Professor of Theology, Jerusalem Seminary; Anglican Chair of Divinity Emeritus, Beeson Divinity School, Samford University), Dr. Timothy Y. Rhee (Truett Theological Seminary), Professor William Mehrens (Distinguished University Professor, Emeritus, Michigan State University), and Rev. Susanne Priddy (Lead Pastor, Wesleyan Chapel United Methodist Church, Wilmington, NC) for their valuable comments and suggestions on this manuscript.

Beyond acknowledgment of the countless sermons that aided in my own spiritual growth, I have been fortunate to have experienced profound, clear, meaningful, and practical sermons in a variety of local church, denominational contexts. Many of the examples and insights in this book have their roots in sermons delivered by Reverend James D. Allen (Dayspring Assembly of God, Bowling Green, OH), Pastor Michael Beasley (Solid Rock Community Church, West Unity, OH), Reverend Buddy Dodge (Church of the Living God, Traverse City, MI), Pastor Jeff Gilmore (Parkview Evangelical Free Church, Iowa City, IA), Father Joe Krupp (Sacred Heart Catholic Church, Hudson, MI), Monsignor Charles Pope (Holy Comforter/St. Cyprian Catholic Church, Washington, DC) and Bud Wrenn (Lead Pastor, Integrity Church, Burlington, NC).

Finally, I am grateful for family members that have helped me in both my writing and spiritual growth. My daughter, Caroline, has been a consistent example of "stretching" to share God's love with others. Although I've not always been their best student, my sons, David and Stephen, have helped me learn many lessons about teaching dos and don'ts in the context of fatherhood and parenting. My wife, Julie, has been a steadfast encourager of my writing and an eagle-eyed editor. I appreciate not only her ability to read my writing and provide objective, honest input from a different perspective ("This part isn't clear. What are you really trying to say here?") but also her constant love, support, and partnership in our own spiritual journey.

I will close this Preface with two important caveats. A critical point about sermons has been made by many writers on this topic. For example, in categorizing the essential ingredients of preaching, Thomas Long identifies four: the congregation, the preacher, the sermon, and the presence of Christ[4]—with those four ingredients having vastly differential ultimate contributions to the efficacy of what is preached.

With regard to Long's fourth point, one thought in particular has helped me keep that focus throughout this book. I have never met Dr. Michael Pasquarello. He currently serves as the Methodist Chair of Divinity, Director of the Robert Smith Jr. Preaching Institute, and Director of Doctor of Ministry at the Beesom Divinity School (Samford University, Birmingham, AL). As I was conceptualizing this book, Dr. Pasquarello and I exchanged a few emails; he freely shared his recommendations for key works in his field that I should be aware of in writing a book on sermons. I learned of many authoritative volumes that have been written about sermons, and I have endeavored not to plow any of that same ground in this book. Embedded in his comments about textbooks on preaching, a single sentence in one of his notes struck me as particularly insightful. He observed that "[M]any of them put almost all the emphasis on the preacher and what the preacher does, rather than God and what God does."[5] This same point has been made in the little collection of preaching tips by Scott Gibson who observed: "When we preach, we want to make an impact on our listeners. That is our ultimate goal. [But] *we* are not the ones who make the impact; *God* ultimately does (2016, p. 19, emphasis added). To those words, I can only add, "Amen!"

A second caveat is this: the avowed intent of this book is to provide insights into how the main ideas of a sermon can best be communicated. The focus is almost exclusively on what the academic field of instructional design has to offer for creating and delivering sermons that offer the best hope of making meaningful differences in the lives of their listeners. On the rare occasion when I might venture into prescriptions for the *content* of a sermon, it is only to illustrate a point about the learning process that is my primary aim. This aim is, however, necessarily secondary to the content. This tenet was brought into crisp focus for me in a conversation with an expert on preaching, Dr. Greg Scharf,[6] who shared with me the following caution: "My own emphasis...has been trying to get preachers to be faithful

---

4. Long, *The Witness of Preaching*, 16-17.

5. Michael Pasquarello, personal communication, September 20, 2019.

6. Greg Sharf, personal communication, January 6, 2022. Dr. Sharf is Professor Emeritus of Homiletics and Pastoral Theology at Trinity Evangelical Divinity School (Deerfield, Illinois) and author of *Let the Earth Hear His Voice*.

Preface

to the biblical text. If they aren't faithful to Scripture, I don't want them to be good teachers or good communicators!"

It is my hope, as the following chapters of this book get into the weeds regarding principles of teaching that can be profitably applied to sermons, that these observations will never leave the forefront. Various bits of what we know from the study of instructional design can help communicate important spiritual truths and can aid in helping listeners to understand and apply them. However, it is Scriptural truth that must be the focus of a sermon, and it is never but God alone who has both authored those truths and his Holy Spirit who makes grasping and applying them possible. It is my hope that to whatever extent the contents of this book may ultimately be useful for preparing or delivering a sermon, they are grounded fully in these realities.

GJC
Chapel Hill, NC

CHAPTER 1

Why Better Sermons?

I IMAGINE THAT A lot of church-going folks have conversations similar to the ones that my wife, Julie, and I often have. Shortly after getting into our car and starting our journey out of the church parking lot on Sunday mornings, we engage in a kind of informal "debriefing" that typically begins with some variant of a basic question: "What did you think of the sermon today?"

Our conversations are often helpful in clarifying what we think we heard; they stimulate deeper consideration of how we believe God is teaching and leading us; they they bring us closer together spiritually.

"That was a really good example he gave about . . ."

"I never thought about . . . that way in my life."

"I didn't understand what he meant about . . ."

"That point about . . . really hit home for me."

That is how our conversations go most of the time. Too often, I think, my wife might ask what key points I took away from the sermon—that concluded only moments earlier—and I am at a loss to even remember the general topic. Often, we both struggle to recall a single key takeaway or to articulate even a vague idea of what the main idea was. That doesn't seem good.

It's not just me. I was comforted to learn that this affliction apparently affects many others. In preparation for writing this book, I ran across the same experience reported by T. David Gordon, a Presbyterian pastor and Professor of New Testament and Greek at Gordon-Conwell Theological Seminary. According to Gordon in his book, *Why Johnny Can't Preach*, "For twenty-five years or more, I routinely have found myself asking my wife, 'What was that sermon about?'—to which she has responded, 'I'm not really sure."[1] (2009, p. 18). In another place, Haddon Robinson relates an anecdote about a U.S. President from the 1920s:

> "Years ago, Calvin Coolidge returned home from services one Sunday and was asked by his wife what the minister talked about. Coolidge replied, 'Sin.' When his wife pressed him as to what the preacher said about sin, Coolidge responded, 'I think he was against it.' The truth is that many people in the pew would not score much higher than Coolidge if quizzed about the content of last Sunday's sermon."[2]

This phenomenon is not unique to me and Calvin Coolidge. Researchers have apparently studied this phenomenon at least on a small scale. In his review of empirical studies of preaching, Clinton Guthrie cites a particularly discouraging study from Germany that found that, less than a day after they heard a sermon sermon, two thirds of those who had an opinion couldn't remember what it was about.[3] In her survey on preaching in America, Lori Carrell asked congregants to "Describe something you gained (or learned) from a specific sermon." Perhaps encouragingly, 68% gave an answer to the question; 32% indicated they could not remember something.[4] I say "perhaps" encouragingly because apparently the survey question did not ask respondents about any sermon in particular (e.g., the sermon last Sunday) but only any specific sermon. Thus, the fact that only 2/3 of respondents could recall something from *any* specific sermon they'd heard seems underwhelming. The fact that approximately 1/3 of respondents couldn't remember something from any specific sermon also seems troubling.

Nor, I suspect, is the phenomenon limited to any individual pastor, specific church, or denomination. My wife and I are veterans of some diverse contexts, ranging from the very non-traditional, free-wheeling, "Jesus People" coffeehouses of the 1970s, to the now-traditional, non-denominational liturgy of contemporary evangelical Protestant services, to the highly traditional orthodoxy of Roman Catholic masses. We've heard many sermons, so we've had many of our debriefing conversations. It's never an exercise in rating a homily as "good" or "bad," or of evaluating a preacher as "strong" or "weak." Rather, our conversations about a sermon are an honest

---

1. Gordon, *Why Johnny Can't Preach*, 18.
2. Robinson, *Biblical Preaching*, 32.
3. Guthrie, "Quantitative Empirical Studies of Preaching," 103.
4. Carrell, *The Great American Sermon Survey*, 91.

yearning to discern a sense of direction and clarify what we think God had wanted us to *learn*.

SERMONS AS TEACHING AND LEARNING EVENTS

Learning. The central theme of this book is learning, and the key takeaway is moving from seeing congregants as listeners to seeing them as learners. Doing so requires at least some attention to the connections between being a preacher and being a teacher. Indeed, Jesus himself was referred to as a "teacher" by both his disciples and those who opposed his ministry.[5] For example, what has come to be known as the "Our Father" prayer was Jesus' response to a request: "Lord, teach us to pray."[6] Jesus was addressed as "Good Teacher" by the rich young man wanting to know how he might inherit eternal life.[7] Opponents such as the Scribes, Pharisees, and Sadducees also used that term to describe Jesus. For example, prefacing their attempt to trap him on the issue of taxation, the Pharisees began: "Teacher, we know that you are a man of integrity and that you teach the way of God in accordance with the truth . . ."[8] It appears that Jesus not only was called "teacher," but he accepted that label. Speaking to his disciples about the role of a servant, he said: "You call me 'Teacher' and 'Lord,' and you are right, because that's what I am."[9] A number of writers have explored Jesus' ministry within the framework of teaching.[10] When asked to choose a word or two to describe their role as preacher, the greatest percentage of respondents in Carrell's survey self-identified as "teacher."[11]

In summary, preaching and teaching aren't the same, but they have a lot in common and it seems likely that what science has found about effective teaching might prove useful in the context of preaching.

---

5. Two caveats are warranted here. First, the same Hebrew word is translated variously as *rabbi* and *teacher*. Second, the exact number of times Jesus is referred to as "teacher" is not known but it is likely close to 60 times in the New Testament, primarily in the gospels.

6. Luke 11:1.

7. Mark 10:17.

8. Matthew 22:16 (NIV).

9. John 13:13.

10. See, for example, Horne, *Jesus, the Master Teacher* and Perkins, *Jesus as Teacher*.

11. Carrell, *The Great American Preaching Survey*, 115.

I will have more to say about learning as a motivation for this book shortly and reconnect with that theme often, but let me first begin by laying out some assumptions about sermons related to learning. For one, I assume that all pastors, deacons, priests, rabbis, shepherds, elders, Sunday school leaders—basically anyone who prepares and delivers any kind of teaching—has as a primary purpose that listeners take away something that has the real potential to change their lives or spur them to action.

My background is in the area of education, where learning is defined in many ways ranging from the social to the neural level. A classic definition of *learning* in the field of educational psychology focuses squarely on experience that leads to change. Learning has been formally defined as a change in behavior that occurs as a result of experience—where that experience is typically exposure to instruction.

I believe that all teachers have as their heart purpose to help others *learn*—that is, to facilitate meaningful changes in not only the lives of those who hear their words, but also via the ripple effects of those changes on the lives of others. Any sermon might certainly be made more memorable via gifted oration; it doesn't seem in itself improper to aspire that listeners find a presentation to be entertaining or, at least, engaging. However, an explicit thesis of this book is that a sermon should be a learning event, comprising memorable content, organized for efficacy by relying on knowledge about learning, and resulting in spiritual growth or change. To focus on that kind of learning is a powerful calling, a vast opportunity, and solemn responsibility that demands great respect and support.

R-E-S-P-E-C-T

A popular song from the late 1960s by the singer regarded as "the Queen of Soul," Aretha Franklin, emphasized the social and personal importance of honoring others. This book is intended to both convey respect for those who prepare and deliver sermons and other teaching events, and to provide support for those efforts.

Regarding respect, much is due. It occurs to me that far too diverse and demanding expectations are placed on the shoulders of many pastors. An individual serving as a pastor, priest, or congregational leader is too often thrust into the contemporaneous roles of organizational head; overseer of budget and finance; marriage, divorce, vocational, grief, abuse and addiction counselor; spiritual guide; school administrator; and—germane to the topic of this book—effective teacher and communicator. It is not surprising that it is difficult to do all of those things well; it would actually be *more* surprising if any single person excelled at all of them.

More realistic, perhaps, is that a person might be gifted in one or two of the areas and struggle with one or more of the others. For example, it seems likely that a pastor might be an insightful, compassionate counselor and successful fundraiser, but have less ability or affection for public speaking. Or, because of preferences or talents, someone might favor leading a senior Bible study or youth group over school administration and organizational leadership tasks. Or vice versa.

Speaking of respect, allow me to digress momentarily to reflect on my decision to write this book. I had some reticence related to the fact that my own familiarity with the art and practice of developing sermons was limited; I didn't want to risk that my work would signal more hubris than helpfulness. But thinking about the powerful discoveries that learning scientists have made and the potential for their application to improve spiritual growth, I concluded that the risk was well worth the reward.

What I can offer are some insights, drawn from what has been learned about how to design an instructional event, that can be easily applied to creating and delivering sermons. I am confident that what science has discovered about how people learn can be profitably applied not just in schools but also in sanctuaries. Why not take advantage of what we know can improve attention, motivation, retention, and application of what any teacher or speaker seeks to communicate? Nearly any sermon plan can be better, and by "better" I mean that it can more effectively stimulate those who engage with a sermon to be more than mere consumers. Invoking the concepts from the first chapter of James' epistle, the aim is to foster not mere hearing of the Word, but doing. A sermon can be designed to help avoid the situation James describes where, as in a mirror, a listener hears, sees truth, but then walks away and forgets.

If it is in the heart of every preacher that his or her words proclaimed on a Sabbath can stimulate meaningful changes in people's lives, then the prospect of deeper, more memorable, and more effectual results along those lines should be appealing. Thus, the primary audience for this book comprises those who teach in any capacity—maybe all of us—and who desire to increase the effectiveness of what we endeavor to share.

Finally, I admit to a lack of formal coursework in homiletics. I have no seminary training. I have no experience as a pastor. In at least three different ways, however, I do come from a position of great experience and an eagerness to support the goals that church leaders have in order to make a difference in people's lives through their teaching.

First, I have spent a career as a teacher myself. My first role was teaching at a small elementary school for five years in northern Michigan. I taught briefly in middle school. I have led Bible studies. I have given over 200 keynote speeches, invited presentations, seminars, and scholarly presentations. I view each of those as teaching opportunities. For approximately the past 30 years, I have been a Professor of Education at the University of Toledo and the University of North Carolina in Chapel Hill, where I have taught undergraduate courses in educational psychology, and graduate-level courses in quantitative research methods, assessment, and program evaluation. I have been deeply immersed in helping others teach and in improving my own teaching for decades.

Second, I have the perspective of someone who has listened attentively from the pews for over 40 years. In that role, I've experienced a *lot* of sermons. Estimating conservatively (i.e., only counting once per week and allowing for a few missed Sundays here and there), that translates into hearing approximately 2,000 sermons.

I took away many things from those sermons. For one thing, appreciation. I am sincerely grateful to the many homilists who risked public speaking in the form of a sermon, because I believe that I learned a good deal from the intended points that they were attempting to convey. For another, my background in research and planning for teaching gave me a meta-cognitive orientation; that is, I have had a focus on thinking about what I was thinking, how I was reacting, why I was thinking and reacting in those ways. Listening through that lens—to sorely mix a metaphor—I took away many insights as to what actions on the part of the speaker prompted me to listen more or less carefully, to focus more or less intently, or to retain more or less of what I was hearing.

Third, as part of my own doctoral training, I gained deep exposure and experience in an academic field called *instructional design*. Instructional design is an area of research and practice, sometimes subsumed by what is called the *learning sciences*, that seeks to discover and apply principles that increase learning.[12] I learned what science had to say about how to organize

---

12. Instructional design has close connections to a number of other related areas such as cognition, learning theory, motivation, memory, and others. To avoid confusion, in this book I'll lump everything under the broad heading of instructional design and not make more nuanced distinctions that would be demanded in an academic work on learning.

and deliver learning interactions so that they were maximally effective in helping students learn. As it turns out, what learning scientists have discovered has many direct applications to developing and delivering sermons. I'm not referring here to fad, popular psychology, but time-tested scientific principles. Nothing along the former lines has found its way into this book. However, it does seem prudent to at least review and evaluate what the learning sciences have to offer. Apparently, that is something that doesn't happen often in the field of homiletics. Guthrie asks—and answers—a relevant question:

> "How much does homiletics engage with contemporary developments in relevant sciences? . . . [T]he evidence indicates that homileticians largely go about their work as though scientific methods and findings are irrelevant to their work. Noticeable by comparison [are] some sister disciplines, such as pastoral care and counseling and congregational studies, which have long relied on empirical methods borrowed from psychology and sociology."[13]

Relevant to the reality that there is only a limited amount of time available in a typical class session, Bible study lesson, or homily—I also gained expertise during my doctoral studies into how to make those interactions as efficient as possible. Early on, I learned and began using often simple-to-incorporate, research-supported strategies that could be implemented to spur learning, to aid in the recall of key ideas, to help my students benefit more from class times, to increase the efficacy of my own teaching, and to aid my students in accomplishing their own goals. The risks of self-examination and modest changes have often yielded substantial benefits to those I have hoped to help.

ACHIEVABLE GOALS

To be sure, this book attempts to walk a fine line. On the one hand, I have admitted that the only experience I have sermonizing is about the same as what most teenagers would say their parents do with regularity. I will avoid addressing that for which I lack adequate knowledge. For example, I won't dip a toe into the deep waters of homiletics, exegesis, hermeneutics, or other aspects of formal seminary training. On the other hand, it is not the goal of this book to reproduce the content of a graduate course in instructional

---

13. Guthrie, "Quantitative Empirical Studies," 68, 70.

design; I promise not to distract from the passionate pursuit of preaching with prescriptive, pedantic principles of an academic area of inquiry.

Reflecting these intentions, this book is not as densely cited with Scriptural teachings as one might expect in a book for Scriptural teachers. It is also (some would hasten to say, "Thankfully!") not densely cited with academic references from the learning sciences, but only what I judged to be essential resources or origins of foundational concepts. When describing and linking academic concepts from the field of instructional design to the development of sermons, I have eschewed invoking scientific vocabulary or technical jargon to communicate about those concepts.[14]

That's what this book is trying *not* to do. What then precisely *are* the goals of this book? Harkening back to the scenario I described earlier of the debriefing conversations between a husband and wife following church attendance on Sunday, the overarching goal of this book is to stimulate curiosity, reflection, and action regarding a specific type of teaching: teaching that has as its purpose imparting spiritual truth and spurring meaningful reflection and concrete changes in people's lives. This book answers three questions: "How can I develop more effective sermons?" "How effective *are* my sermons?" "How do I know?"

Assuming as I do that those who are called to teaching earnestly desire to reach their audiences with perspective- and life-changing messages, the practical goal of this book is to provide some strategies to accomplish that. The following chapters provide actionable ways to answer the question, "How can consideration of instructional design principles help my sermons have greater impact?"

I am especially optimistic about the potential for greater impact because I believe that nearly all readers will find some *very* easily-adapted ideas to incorporate in their lessons, sermons, and so on. Moreover, I believe that even modest incorporation of these ideas will reward the effort, resulting in noticeable listener engagement, encouraging feedback, and positive evidence of effectiveness.

All sermons *can* be better in terms of provoking great engagement, recall, and application of their intended messages. We want hearers not merely to listen, but to learn.

However, the goals just identified can't be accomplished by the mechanical incorporation of "teaching tips," the latest multi-media technology,

---

14. As will be seen in Chapter 3, I both recommend this posture and provide rationales and examples for embracing it also in the development of sermons.

or a cookie cutter, checklist approach. Indeed, in style and content, this book purposefully avoids prescriptive, one-size-fits-all recipes and simplistic "how-to" formulations. As others have cautioned, there are sober reasons for avoiding such an approach: "If we concentrate on trying to make a certain aspect of things 'work', it will become a formula for us and will only lead us into bondage."[15]

Sermons that make a difference in listeners' lives begin with many elements not addressed in this book—and certainly of higher priority than many of the ideas presented here. Sermons that make a difference require purposeful, sustained attention to many factors, including one's own spiritual life, the unique needs of a specific congregation, and immersion in Scripture. Even the most well-designed sermon is likely to lack effect—or even cause harm—absent the leading and presence of the Holy Spirit. As Robinson has noted: "Ultimately, the authority behind preaching resides not in the preacher but in the biblical text."[16] Accordingly, I acknowledge that the content of this book seems trivial compared to these deeper concerns. That said, however, there *are* practical matters that, if attended to, can improve the reach, retention, and resonance of any sermon.

SO BUCKLE UP

As indicated previously, I begin with an assumption that those who are called to teaching earnestly desire to reach their audiences with perspective- and life-changing messages. We *want* preaching to be more effective. But wanting to deliver better sermons is not enough, and the ideas covered in this book are perhaps the easiest part. What may be the more challenging part in the pursuit of better teaching is that it requires a posture of humility and courage.

The need for humility and courage was made clear to me in one of my own first experiences learning to be an elementary school teacher. I had taken a position as a second grade teacher and I was encouraged by a mentor, Professor Stephen Yelon of Michigan State University, to tape record myself—yes, the technology of tape recording dates this experience to the early 1980s!—as I taught my group of second graders. Before my students arrived for school that morning, I loaded a portable cassette recorder with the longest tape available at the time (120 minutes), placed the recorder

15. Quoted in Hession and Hession, *We Would See Jesus*, 7.
16. Robinson, *Biblical Preaching*, p. 23.

on a shelf behind my desk, and pushed PLAY. The tape rolled for the next two hours and, after school had ended for the day, I sat down for a personal debriefing session pertaining to my own teaching.

What I learned by listening carefully (and privately) to the tape was both humbling and embarrassing, but also immensely helpful. In the following paragraphs, I'll describe a few examples of what I discovered. To be more precise, the following provide examples of what had already been discovered by learning scientists but were then becoming salient for me. These examples are not necessarily related to how one might prepare and deliver a sermon (but they could be). Rather, they are intended primarily to illustrate the kind of straightforward, clear principles that the field of instructional design and related research have to offer—and to serve as an advance warning regarding the kind of frank feedback that such self-examination can provide.

Principle 1: Avoid things that take away from what you are trying to communicate.

The first—and glaringly obvious as I listened to the tape recording—thing that I discovered in my debriefing was a previously unknown distracting habit: I said "uh" a lot. How had I not been aware of that before? Listening to the audio, I made a list with a checkmark for each time I said "uh" when giving directions for a mathematics activity.

Me: "Please put away your art supplies now and, *uh*, ✓ I'd like each of you to, *uh*, ✓ take out a sheet of, *uh*, ✓ paper and, *uh*, ✓ a pencil."

I counted dozens of checkmarks on my list. Just hearing myself made me cringe—but also, thankfully, I became aware of a distracting habit that must have driven my students crazy and diverted attention from the content I was trying to teach.

Principle 2: More learning occurs when people are empowered as active listeners and participants.

For the social studies portion of our class that day, I did a separate analysis of the percentage of time I was talking versus the amount of time students were actively, verbally engaged in class discussions. It was not a good ratio. It was particularly discouraging considering that getting students to wrestle with the questions they were having about the content and more actively participate in the discussion had been my goal for deciding to have a discussion in the first place. In truth, it was more of a monologue

Why Better Sermons?

than a discussion. I dominated the classroom discourse and afforded students few opportunities to meaningfully join in, few opportunities to ask questions, try out some of their own ideas, or become invested participants in what I'd hoped we'd be learning that day.

Principle 3: When asking a question, allow some "wait time" for responses.

In that same social studies lesson, I also discovered that, when I did ask a question hoping for students to engage in a discussion, I typically allowed virtually no time for them to formulate responses or clarifying questions. The lesson went something like this:

> Me: "What do you think are some things that people most need? *[almost no pause]*. Well, how about shelter for one thing? People can't live outside in the heat, rain, and snow and all that. Food is pretty important, isn't it? *[no pause]* If we didn't have food, we couldn't survive, could we? *[no pause]*. Water, too, right? Anything else? *[another no pause]* What about other people to love and care for them?" Is that important? *[no pause]* Sure it's important. Or, what about transportation—ways for people to get from one place to another? *[no pause]* Any other ideas?"

Since that awful discussion (and it would be ideal here if I could use the visual gesture of putting air quotes around the word "discussion" to indicate sarcasm), I've tried to implement a simple but effective strategy to turn air-quoted discussions into authentic learning events. There is a long-established and pretty straightforward instructional design principle called *wait time*. Whenever asking questions such as I was posing to my students, it's important to allow them even a few precious seconds to contemplate the question and begin to think about a response. Estimates of the appropriate amount of wait time vary, but as little as five seconds can be enormously beneficial for student learning. Five seconds might *seem* like a very brief amount of time but try it sometime. Ask a question, then wait. Make an important point in a sermon, then pause, allow some silence, and wait for learners to consider it. Five seconds of silence seems like an eternity particularly if, like me, you have the "no pause" penchant.

The science isn't totally prescriptive on the topic of wait time, however. It's likely not something that should be done following every question or key point, and it's unclear exactly what the sweet spot is in terms of amount of time to wait. As an upper bound, more than 15 seconds is probably too much (and *super* awkward). Five seconds is probably a good lower bound. Just that much would have been substantially more generous and helpful than the two nanoseconds I was shocked to learn that I was typically affording for my students to process a question, contemplate its content, and consider a response.

Principle 4: Name first, then question.

This is a very early finding and probably one of the simplest and most effective ways to help people connect to a discussion (and to avoid embarrassment). In listening to the audio tape of my teaching, I discovered that I had a habit of phrasing questions so that they ended with the name of the student I was hoping to answer the question. For example, I might ask: "Of all the things we just listed, like shelter, food, and water, which thing do you think is the most important need people have, *Jeremy*?" I have no idea why this didn't occur to me naturally, but listening to my tape-recorded lesson, it was a revelation to hear the shock in Jeremy's voice—or for that matter the surprise nearly every student exhibited when I would ask a question followed by the name of the student I was calling on. I found myself routinely having to repeat questions (and wondering to myself why Jeremy and the other students hadn't been paying better attention!).

But the real culprit was *me*. I was the one who hadn't been paying close enough attention to simple principles of instruction—until I heard my own teaching. In this case, the principle is well-established: People can best focus on the question and provide a thoughtful response when they hear their name first, *then* the question. This alerts the listener, allows them to attend to the question from the beginning, avoids surprising or embarrassing them at being asked to contribute, and jump starts the process of thinking about a response or asking for relevant clarifying information. I wouldn't have shocked Jeremy—and, importantly, he would almost certainly have *learned* and contributed more—had I simply rephrased my question as: "So, Jeremy, of all the things we just listed like shelter, food, and water, which thing do you think is the most important need people have?"

THE JOURNEY AHEAD

Although they apply in a vast variety of situations, the foregoing four examples were not directed explicitly to the context of delivering sermons or lessons in a church-related setting. Identifying personal distracting behaviors can help when addressing the finance committee. Monitoring how much talking we're doing versus how much others are doing can be helpful in counseling sessions. Affording some wait time and using name-first questioning can help in child rearing and countless other contexts.

These examples of pragmatic principles were provided mainly to illustrate the kind of practical strategies that have resulted from the work of those engaged in the field of instructional design. They were also provided for the purpose of foreshadowing the kinds of application-oriented examples that will be presented in the remainder of this book. I believe that readers will find many of the ideas to come just as simple, easy-to-implement, and effective as the preceding four principles.

Additionally, we will be leaving the context of my second grade classroom and, in the subsequent chapters of this book, focusing exclusively on in-depth examples of specific principles that have a more direct and obvious relationship to the context of preparing and delivering sermons. Because this is not a book on the academic topic of instructional design but a book intended to encourage more effective teaching in the context of spiritual growth, from this point forward I will only occasionally make any references to the research underlying the principles that will be presented.[17] Instead, this book will present ideas for improving sermons that are based on what works, with specific examples to illustrate those ideas. Also included at relevant junctures will be cautions about common mistakes and "non-examples" (often drawn from my own foibles) of how *not* to do something.

A final thought on courage and humility. Both of those attributes are essential to engaging in the kind of self-examination that leads to insights such as these about one's own teaching. Technology has come a long way since my use of cassette tape replay and, as we will see in Chapter 6, reliance on even the most up-to-date technologies is not the most potent way to engage in such examination. Beyond the presumed commitment to have a greater impact on people's spiritual lives, the courage to even begin the journey is likely the most important personal attribute required. It was hard—but worthwhile—to hear (and revise) some of my embarrassing tendencies on that tape. How much more worthwhile might it be to

---

17. For the reader who is interested in more on the topic of instructional design, several classic, scholarly and practical reference works authored by a mentor for my own teaching are available. See, for example, Yelon, *Powerful Principles of Instruction*.

understand and address aspects that limit the effectiveness of the sermons we develop and deliver.

CONCLUSIONS

The answer to the question posed in the title of this chapter, "Why better sermons?," is probably obvious. The potential for making a greater difference in people's lives is surely the most fundamental reason for our goal of better sermons. I suspect that anyone reading this book already possesses the requisite qualities of courage and humility, so the upcoming journey to better sermons will be challenging but enlightening and gratifying. Godspeed on our journey!

In closing, let me return to the Sunday morning debriefing conversations described at the beginning of this chapter. I don't think that my wife and I are the only ones having such conversations. We appreciate the preparation, patience, and pastoral care of those who preach. Those of us who hear a sermon on any given Sunday *want* to grasp more of what was intended, to apply key lessons learned in practical ways in our everyday lives, and to fully embrace and deeply understand eternal truths in ways that we can share them with others. We are eager that He who began a good work in us will be faithful to complete it. We *want* to learn.

As a fellow teacher concerned with supporting meaningful changes in people's lives via our teaching, I share a common sadness with preachers when *anyone* heads home without a clear grasp of what I had hoped to convey, without a crisp sense of how that teaching can be applied in their lives, or sometimes even without recalling the main idea of a presentation. All of that can easily change. To a substantial degree, reconceptualizing sermons as learning events and all that entails can help listeners understand, learn, apply, and recall sermon content in ways that facilitate spiritual change and growth. All sermons *can* be better. We now turn to some concrete ways to help make that happen.

CHAPTER 2

Are You Ready?

I DON'T RECALL WHERE I first saw the cliche at the end of this paragraph. I have a vague sense that it might have been on the television show, The Office. The office manager, Michael Scott—among other grating characteristics—had an irritating compulsion for implementing the MBA fad-of-the-moment. The one that sticks in my mind involves one of those saccharine attempts at motivational messaging in the form of a colorful wall poster that proclaims: "Luck Is What Happens When Preparation Meets Opportunity!"

The ostensible rationale for such posters is to get employees fired up about their jobs, to encourage them to take risks, to put their noses to grindstones, to work as a team, and to adopt other virtuous workplace behaviors. Michael Scott wanted his employees to get the training, skills, and perspectives they needed so that they would be ready when a fertile sales prospect appeared, with the ultimate goal of increasing company profits. In reality, of course, the motivational quote isn't about luck at all. Just the opposite.

In searching for the origin of that saying, I found that it is often sourced to a historical figure named Seneca (aka, "Lucius Annaeus Seneca" and "Seneca the Younger"). Seneca lived in the early first century in Rome; he came from a wealthy family and was regarded as a thinker, an orator, a teacher of rhetoric, and a politician. Today, he is perhaps best known as a philosopher—a field of study he undertook during a period of exile later in his life. The then-Emperor of Rome, Claudius, banished Seneca to the island of Corsica as a result of Seneca's alleged adultery with Claudius' niece. (There are two side observations to be made here, somewhat tongue-in-cheek. First, how much of a deep thinker or politically-savvy could Seneca really have been if he lacked enough sense to avoid getting involved with the Emperor's niece? Second, although Corsica has some appeal today as a lovely vacation destination, it must have been a much less desirable spot in the first century if people were banished there to study philosophy.)

Figure 2-1

Lucius Annaeus Seneca

On a more serious note, Seneca was, in reality, apparently mocking the notion of luck in the quote attributed to him. Rather than good outcomes being the result of chance or serendipity, they are more rationally attributable to the hard work that cultivates the abilities needed for success. Those abilities can then be applied at whatever fortuitous junctures that present themselves. Essentially the same sentiment is expressed in the saying "You make your own luck" or more aphoristically two millennia since Seneca in the familiar motto that encouraged Boy Scouts to "Be Prepared."

It would be unfortunate to be a person who falls into a crevice and is injured while on a mountain trail hike. It would be fortunate if that person's companion was an Eagle Scout who could prepare a bowline knot at the end of a rope to reach and rescue the fallen hiker. But lashing the appropriate knot isn't a matter of good or bad fortune; it doesn't happen by accident; and it can't be tied with any amount of "good luck" if the Eagle Scout hadn't already mastered it. In fact, that particular type of knot is probably not one that many readers have ever even heard of, much less, attempted to master. (For anyone curious, Figure 2-2 shows the five steps involved in tying the bowline knot.) To be sure, situations requiring skill in tying a bowline knot may not be encountered more than a handful of times over a lifetime of hiking, but "luck" would have nothing to do with using that skill to effect a rescue: it would be the preparation and practice that came in handy at the opportune time.

Figure 2-2

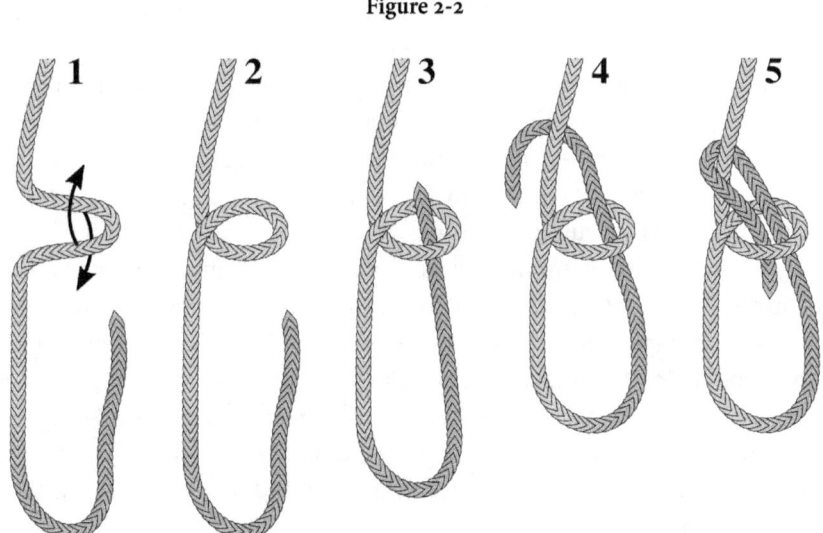

Bowline Knot-Tying Steps

TURNING APTITUDE INTO SKILL

Of course, anyone who delivers a sermon or teaches a group already knows that it takes preparation. I've never prepared a formal sermon, but in my own career as a university professor, my experience is that, if I will be covering a new topic next week, it takes me at least 8-12 hours of preparation to prepare an hour-long lecture I haven't given previously. Respondents to Carrell's survey estimated that it takes their pastors about 12 hours to prepare a sermon; this was close to the pastors own estimates of the time required (about 9 hours).[1] The short duration given to actually delivering a sermon pales in comparison: research reported in 2019 based on a review of nearly 50,000 sermons found that sermons typically average only 37 minutes.[2] Carrell's survey found that both pastors and congregants believed even less time was optimal. When asked their ideas about the ideal sermon length, Catholic listeners reported that about 15 minutes was ideal (Catholic priests said that 9 minutes was optimal). Respondents from Protestant congregations thought 25 minutes was best on average which was close to the 22 minutes which was the opinion of Protestant ministers. In both cases, sermon delivery takes far less time than sermon preparation. An appropriate parallel is one my wife reminds me of: it requires days of preparation to host a Thanksgiving meal that takes only an hour or so to consume!

To the extent that students' evaluations of my teaching are a valid indication, I am generally regarded as a good teacher. I am thankful for the gift of aptitude for teaching. Importantly, however, uncultivated aptitude rarely develops into a skill. Whatever talent for teaching I possess has resulted from not only the gift, but also from the grit. Teaching is hard work, requiring—at least for me—a substantial investment of time for focused, thoughtful, and meticulous planning.

What kind of planning is necessary and most effective? In the following sections of this chapter, we'll move from a general acknowledgement of the importance of preparation to consideration of some specific aspects of preparation that can help make sermons have a greater impact on their intended audiences. The impact that I'll be prioritizing—learning—is characterized not only cognitive understanding of what was intended to be communicated, but by the changes in heart, mind, and actions that flow from that understanding.

---

1. Carrell, *The Great American Sermon Survey*, 86, 108

2. Regarding the 37-minute average, the data on sermon length come from a report by the Pew Research Center, "The Digital Pulpit." Researchers transcribed a sample of 49,719 sermons delivered between April 7 and June 1, 2019, and made available online. It is unclear how representative the sample was; the authors indicate that sermons were drawn from a sample of 6,431 churches located primarily in urban areas and having larger-than-average congregations. The median sermon length was 37 minutes, although there were substantial differences across differing traditions. Of the four categories of religious tradition, Catholic sermons tended to be the shortest (median length of 14 minutes); sermons given in historically Black Protestant churches tended to be the longest (median = 54 minutes); sermons in mainline Protestant churches and evangelical Protestant churches averaged between those extremes at 25 and 39 minutes, respectively.

ASPECTS OF PREPARATION

In the sections that follow, five aspects of preparation will be presented. Some of the following might seem obvious at first. However, deeper reflection on even things that might seem obvious on the surface can yield insights that would not be immediately apparent if the "obviousness" induced lesser attention to them. In some ways, this focus on fundamentals in successful sermon preparation is similar to successful preparation in other areas. Coaches and elite athletes are sometimes asked about the reasons for their success. It is not uncommon for them to reveal that they drill, coach, and practice "the fundamentals" and to attribute their success in large part to that focus. When success is elusive in elementary education, school districts often go "back to basics." A prominent scholarly journal in religious studies proclaims a focus on *First Things*.

In addition to presenting what may seem to be some obvious, commonsense principles, additional sections will address other aspects that may not naturally occur when thinking about sermon preparation. Finally, I note that the following sections will *not* address preparation style or habits. As much as science can inform the development of better sermons, their creation and execution are also to some extent artistic and matters of great individual differences. A style that might be highly successful for one person may not work at all for another. Habits of preparation such as setting aside extensive, fixed blocks of time versus preparing in shorter, flexible "bursts" vary according to personality, preference, and penchant. The following sections will instead focus on ideas that can be adapted to any individual style.

Nevermind "Thyself"

"Know Thyself." It is likely that every reader of this book has heard this saying. Its familiarity and ubiquity probably contribute to its aura of gravity (and the fact that it's old, dating back to approximately the 4th century BC). It is one of 147 *apophthegmata*[3]—pithy words of advice—inscribed on a stone monument at the temple of Apollo, the ancient Greek god of

---

3. In a subsequent chapter, I'll recommend eschewing the temptation to invoke Greek, Hebrew, Aramaic, or other foreign or ancient languages, or limiting such to only when absolutely necessary to convey meaning. Here, the use of a Greek term is probably unnecessary. If a reader concludes that I included it only to convey a false impression regarding the depth of my own liberal education and scholarly moorings, such a conclusion would be reasonable.

music, harmony, and light. "Know Thyself" is one of what are considered to be three higher-order apophthegmata, with the others being "Nothing to Excess" and "Surety Brings Ruin." These "Big Three" maxims may also have attained that status because of their relatively non-controversial and timeless nature. This is in contrast to some of the other 147 that are obscure, overlooked, and essentially never cited, such as "Control Your Marriages," "Rule Your Wife," "Associate with Likeminded People," and "Honor the Hearth."

The impulse to gain self-knowledge certainly has some historical longevity to the extent that urgings and methods for doing so extend from the Apollonic temple etchings of 2500 years ago to contemporary passions to probe one's enneagram or Myers-Briggs type. I suspect that gaining deeper self-awareness may be good advice generally and may have some role to play in giving better sermons. However, the first key aspect of preparation to be examined here reflects precisely the opposite advice: "Know Thy Audience."

Figure 2-3

Know Thy Audience

The first consideration in developing an effective sermon is evaluating the characteristics, backgrounds, interests, and needs of the intended audience. Robinson has put the priority this way: "Preaching is fundamentally a part of the care of souls, and the care of souls involves a thorough understanding of the congregation."[4]

I can speak firsthand of the disasters I've experienced when I've presented a heavily technical presentation to a non-technical audience or when I've presented a non-technical address to a highly technical group. I've had references to the comedy of Keegan-Michael Key and Jordan Peele be unrecognized by a group of boomers, and I've gotten blank stares from

---

4. Robinson, *Biblical Preaching*, 78.

today's college students when I've alluded to the Bass-o-Matic of Saturday Night Live notoriety. Some sermon audiences will immediately understand the significance of "raising an Ebenezer"; for other audiences, only a puzzled sense about the relevance of parenting Charles Dickens' Scrooge might come to mind.

Many characteristics can be relevant to consider; precisely which ones are most important to consider in a given situation requires some reflection on the purpose and content of the sermon being prepared. Table 2-1 provides a starting point for such consideration. Regardless of the specific topic of a sermon, it is important to consider the audience characteristics shown in the table—and others—and to keep those characteristics in mind so that main ideas, allusions, examples, and specific vocabulary used in a sermon will be accessible to all listeners.

Table 2-1
Some Learner Characteristics to Consider in Sermon Development

Characteristic	*Implication: Differential familiarity with . . .*
Age	references to historical events (e.g., the Great Depression, the Vietnam War, Civil Rights marches, 9/11)
Technological Savvy	tech-originating concepts ("Just ping him for that information." "It just blew my buffer." Pixels. Apps. Zoom. Podcasts.)
Sex	predominately male/female or traditionally gender-specific activities, roles, or perspectives
Residence	community or area history, landmarks, events
Socio-economic Status (SES)	contexts, activities, and perspectives associated with wealth or poverty (e.g., 401k, SNAP benefits, bull or bear markets)
Cultural Knowledge	allusions to historical or contemporary literature, music, movies, games (board/video), television shows, artists
Education Level	vocabulary, academic coursework, post-secondary schooling contexts
Spiritual Development	content of the Bible, experience of sacraments, church history and traditions, knowledge of specific martyrs, saints, preachers, and doctrinal statements
Hobbies/Interests	sports, gardening, literature, cooking, travel

What's the Point?

A second, and perhaps seemingly obvious point is that a sermon should have one. No disrespect is intended here, so please bear with the point of this section. I am not the first to highlight this admonition; it appears often enough in advice about preaching that it likely bears repeating as a first principle. The point has been made in several ways:

According to Donald G. Miller, "any single sermon should have just one major idea."[5]

Robinson has asserted that "a central, unifying idea must be at the heart of an effective sermon."[6]

Referring to what he called *unity* in a sermon, Presbyterian theologian Robert Dabney[7] was clearly describing the necessity of suffusing a sermon with focus on a main point:

> "Unity requires two things. The speaker must, first, have one main subject of discourse to which he adheres with supreme reference throughout. But this is not enough. He must, second, propose to himself one definite impression on the hearer's soul, to the making of which everything in the sermon is bent." (1870, p. 109)

In his guide to famous theologians, Gerald McDermott describes Anglican priest and (later) Catholic priest and cardinal John Henry Newman as "rightly famous for his preaching" and Newman's insistence that "preachers should focus on only one point in each sermon."[8]

There is also some empirical support for these admonitions. For example, a random sample of members of 15 Roman Catholic parishes and based on sermons delivered by 26 different priests, parishioners responded to a brief survey on sermon impact. Statistical analysis revealed that, while the strongest predictor of a sermon's impact was its perceived relevance

---

5. Miller, *The Way to Biblical Preaching*, 53.

6. Robinson, *Biblical Preaching*, 35.

7. Robert Lewis Dabney was an American theologian, Presbyterian pastor, architect, chaplain in the Confederate army and biographer of Stonewall Jackson. Although his theological writings were influential, his legacy as a Christian apologist has diminished as a result of his support for slavery, opposition to public education, and his perspectives on other social issues. The quote is from his work, *Sacred Rhetoric; or, A Course of Lectures on Preaching*, 109.

8. McDermott, *The Great Theologians*, 156.

to the listeners' lives. Coming in a strong second was the extent to which listeners could discern the main idea of the sermon.[9]

There are many suggestions, templates, and strategies that have been proposed by others for helping a preacher organize his or her thinking about a sermon's main point (or points). Because the focus in this book is not to dwell on specific techniques, I'll mention only one that provides an illustration of the kinds of organizing approaches that exist. Figure 2-4 shows the "Application Grid" method developed by 9Mark Ministries.[10] The grid provides a structured approach for developing the main point or subpoints of a sermon around six areas. The *Unique Salvation History* column can be used to consider how a key point relates to redemption history. The *Non-Christian* column prompts consideration of how one of the points has implications for unbelievers. The *Public* column can be used to record thoughts about one or more points related to believers' approaches to public life (e.g., the law, the community, personal finances, politics, employment). The *Christ* column can be used to elaborate on the meaning of key points vis a vis how listeners relate to the Lord. The fifth column, *Individual Christian*, can be used to consider implications of the key points for discipleship. The final column, *Local Church*, prompts consideration of how the sermon's key points relate to the life of the local congregation.

In short, the most important point of a sermon should be a focal target that is kept sharply salient throughout sermon development and presentation. The primary question that should serve not only the starting point but frequent touchstone is this: "*What is the most essential thing that I'd like listeners to take away from my sermon?*"

---

9. Pargament and Silverman, "Exploring Some Correlates of Sermon Impact on Catholic Parishioners."

10. The grid shown in the figure does not contain any notes or entries; an example of a completed grid can be found at https://anglicanexpositor.files.wordpress.com/2011/10/application-grid.pdf

Sermon Science

Figure 2-4

	Unique Salvation History	Non-Christian	Public	Christ	Unity in Diversity	Work	Gender/ Marriage/ Family	Individual Christian	Your Local Church
Main Point #1									
Sub Point #2.A									
Sub Point #2.B									
Sub Point #2.B.1									
Sub Point #2.B.2									
Sub Point #2.B.3									
Sub Point #2.B.4									
Conclusion									

Text: _____ Sermon Title: _____ Date Preached: _____

KEY
Unique Salvation History—What about the passage is important for the way God unfolds his plan of salvation in history? What's unrepeatable by us but worthy of worshipping God for or needing further explanation?
Non-Christian—How does the passage speak to the unbeliever? How does it call him/her to repentance and belief? How does it warn, rebuke, correct, or prod the unbeliever? What does it say about the danger of the unbeliever's situation, the exclusivity of Christ, the sinner's need for a Savior, or the sufficiency of that Savior as a substitute for the sinner?
Public—What does the passage say about our lives and roles in the public sphere, both as Christians and non-Christians (e.g. government, neighborhood)?
Christ—How is Jesus foreshadowed or typed? What particular perfection of Christ does that type depict? How is Jesus remembered or described in character, authority, glory, or essence?
Unity in Diversity—How does this passage demonstrate the unity that we have in Christ? How does it reflect the diversity of the body?
Work—What does this passage say to the employee and employer?
Gender/Marriage/Family—How does the passage speak to men? How does the passage speak to women? How does this passage apply to the husband and wife and how does this apply to the family?
Individual Christian—What does the passage mean for the life of the individual Christian? How does it call him/her to deeper repentance and belief? How does it warn, rebuke, correct, motivate, comfort or encourage the Christian?
Your Local Church—What does the passage mean for the corporate life of our local church? How does it call the local corporate body to tend to its corporate life together and corporate witness to the unbelieving community around it?

9Mark Ministries Application Grid

In reconceptualizing listeners as learners, it also becomes clear that developing and delivering a sermon with even a single main point in mind is not enough. This is key: The point that a pastor has in mind must be the point that the listeners have in mind—that is, the main idea that they receive, engage with, and remember.

The phrasing of the primary question just identified is not prescriptive, only illustrative. There are many ways to frame the same basic question:

- "What is the one idea that I'd most want people to remember from this sermon?"
- "Of all the points to be made in this sermon, which is most important?"
- "What hoped-for change in listener's lives, hearts, actions, habits, attitudes, or behaviors is the central focus of this sermon?"

The main point to be taken from this section is that the main point of a sermon should be established—in as concrete a manner as possible—as one of the first steps in sermon preparation.

In the preface to this volume, I committed that I would not reduce important ideas to a tightly prescribed list of tips and techniques. This first recommendation gets as close as I will to violating that commitment, but for good reason. The recommendation is that the main point of a sermon should be explicitly shared with listeners at the beginning of a sermon. There is good reason for this recommendation. As will be described in a following section, "Linking to the Point," clear, upfront communication of the intended main point(s) provides a kind of mental framework for listeners that fosters better understanding and recall.

Additionally, the main point should be revisited at various junctures during the sermon delivery. Repetition is often highly beneficial or even essential to learning. Regarding explicit communication of the intended main point of a sermon, however, the *mechanics* of this repetition are not essential. The main point may be alluded to verbatim at various times during the sermon; it might instead be referenced in a rephrasing, paraphrasing, or presented in a different mode (e.g., visual, text, audio) at appropriate intervals in the sermon. The bottom line is that the burden of trying to discern the main point is not something listeners should have to wrestle with, or a responsibility placed on them; it should be explicitly provided from the outset of a sermon.

Getting to the Point

There are likely many paths that an inspiration, event, experience, Scripture, or kernel of an idea for a sermon can take to arrive at a single, clear, specific main idea. To aid in that development, I will suggest that getting to the point of having a focused, intended main idea nearly always benefits from the preacher's struggle of reducing the seminal idea to a single, written sentence. Coming up with that single topic sentence may, in fact, be the most arduous—but most consequential—activity in preparing a sermon. Working on a presentation without developing a clear, focused main idea can yield a sermon, but risks failing to aid listeners in grasping what was intended. This point was made succinctly by Robinson: "A mist in the pulpit becomes a fog in the pew."[11]

Going from conceptualizing the intent of a sermon to actually stating a main point in writing is a process that results in added clarity, refines the initial idea, and a specific purpose then is available to guide all subsequent decisions, such as decisions about which examples to use, which Scriptural references are most relevant, which anecdotes to relate, which supporting points are appropriate, and so on. Actually, forcing oneself to draft, revise, edit, finalize a specific *written* intended point has many subtle benefits for advancing the listeners' learning, understanding, or changes in behavior that motivated the sermon idea in the first place.

Two situations illustrate this aspect of preparation. The first, somewhat extended, example comes from my experience as a faculty advisor for doctoral students who are considering the final step in their PhD program: conducting a research study for their dissertation. It is not uncommon for me to meet with a student after he or she has completed all of their doctoral coursework and to discuss what their dissertation research topic might be. I actually had a student once—and thankfully, only one!—say that she was thinking of doing something "on education." I knew from her class performance and other evidence that she was an insightful and promising student—but one who had not yet thought carefully about the specific focus of her dissertation research. It required several more conversations for us to hone-in on a specific topic. The following snippets trace those conversations over an extended number of meetings. The abridged version of those conversations related here—compiled across several meetings—doesn't fully convey the struggles we faced to go from a good, general idea to a specific topic. Hopefully, however, it does illustrate what I mean by starting with a general idea and working toward a single, elaborated sentence that captures a complete well-formed main idea that could be used as a launching point for a dissertation—or a sermon.

> Me: *"I understand you're interested in something on education? That's great, but what area related to education?"*
>
> Student: *"Well, I was thinking of something to do with education for special needs students."*

11. Robinson, *Biblical Preaching*, 141.

Me: *"What kinds of special needs?"*

Student: *"When I volunteered as a tutor, I really felt called to work with students that maybe have learning disabilities."*

Me: *"But there are lots of different types of learning disabilities, right? Are you most interested in visual impairment? Dyslexia? Auditory processing difficulties? Something else?"*

Student: *"I was actually thinking about ADHD [attention deficit, hyperactivity disorder]."*

Me: *"Oh, good! That's an important area, and I know there is a lot that needs to be investigated. Off the top of my head, I wonder if you are thinking of looking at the physiology of ADHD, or pharmacological treatments, or behavioral therapies? And are you interested in researching ADHD for a specific subject area or at a specific grade level?"*

Student: *"Well, no. Not really any of those."*

Me: *"What then?"*

Student: *Hmmm . . . I guess that from my work at Nathan Middle School. I've kind of noticed that it seems like boys are more often referred by their teachers for ADHD diagnosis and treatment than girls are. From my reading about ADHD in our courses, it doesn't seem like there is a sex-linked reason for that disparity, so I was wondering if maybe there are some social or cultural factors at play."*

Me: *"Perfect! So your main focus would be something along these lines: To what extent do social or cultural factors explain differential ADHD referral rates for middle school aged boys and girls? Does that get at what you're thinking?"*

Student: *"Yes! That's exactly it!"*

In the end, the student developed what was one of the most interesting and useful dissertation studies with which I've been associated. Over the several weeks reflected in the dialogue above, it wasn't an easy process to reduce her general education topic to a single, specific, well-defined question, but the effort paid off. The final product was a study that investigated the extent to which teachers who are presented with certain in-class behaviors (e.g., fidgeting, acting out, interrupting, distractibility) are more likely to view those behaviors as indicators of ADHD when demonstrated by middle school aged boys than when demonstrated by middle school aged girls.

That topic was both highly important (that is, if there was differential teacher response to the same behaviors in boys and girls, that might shed light on why more boys than girls were typically referred by teachers for further evaluation for ADHD and why more boys than girls ended up with the ADHD label) and crisply focused (that is, having that concrete topic statement in hand provided a clear guide for making all subsequent decisions, such as who should be involved in the study, how to design the study, what research procedures and analyses should be used, and so on).

The final study ended up presenting a sample of teachers with descriptions of students and asking the teachers to evaluate whether they believed the students might benefit from referral and treatment for ADHD. Two student profiles were created; both had the same descriptions of student behaviors in terms of grades, attendance, age, and so on; both used student names that could be interpreted as either a boy or a girl (e.g., Chris, Pat). The only—and significant—difference in the profiles was that one profile explicitly identified "Chris" as a girl; the parallel profile identified Chris as a boy. Teachers read and evaluated a randomly assigned profile. My student learned that the sex of a student was a significant factor in whether a teacher perceived a student to have ADHD symptoms and in whether teachers saw a need for further evaluation and treatment.

Why have I related that example in depth here? Three implications of this example are noteworthy. First, it was a struggle to move from the general topic of wanting to do something in the area of education to the highly-focused main idea. It is always easier to just have a topic in mind than it is to actually write it out as a single sentence. In my experience with planning and presenting any lesson, the act of writing it as a complete sentence that attempts to articulate a succinct, focused main idea almost always progresses in similar way as the topic refinement dialogue that occurred with the graduate student—in fits and starts, but ending in a very helpful place.

Second, the benefit of struggling to distill a general topic into a specific main idea will be realized in the comparative ease with which subsequent preparation decisions fall into line. Getting to the point of settling—ideally in writing—on a highly-specific topic provides the roadmap for all the decision points and preparations that follow. For example, topic specificity stimulates reflection on how to narrow the idea, which essential aspects of the topic to address, what is most (and least) relevant for inclusion, what examples might be helpful, which audience characteristics are most important, and so on.

Finally, if the preacher can't derive a single, focused sentence that captures the main idea of a sermon, how can the listeners be expected to do so? How could they be expected to learn, understand, and apply what they are hearing in that situation? Writing directly to preachers, Robinson suggested:

> "Those who hear you do not understand what you are saying unless they can answer the basic questions: What is the preacher talking about today? What is he saying about what he is talking about?". . . Sunday after Sunday men and women leave church unable to state the preacher's basic idea because the preacher has not bothered to state it himself."[12]

The example presented earlier based on my experience of struggling with a student to develop the main idea for dissertation research was taken from the context with which I am most familiar. But I also have substantial experience with the same phenomenon as a listener to sermons. Like Coolidge's recollection of "sin" as the main point of a sermon, I have sometimes been left with only the vaguest sense of an admonition to "be more heavenly minded"—or similar ephemeral notion that lacks much specificity or staying power.

For example, I have heard many sermons that began something along the lines of "Today, I'd like to talk about holiness." An important topic to be sure, but not a specific main idea to be grasped or retained. Consequently, when my wife and I have engaged in our post-service sermon conversations on the way home, we'll most likely recall that the sermon was "something about holiness." We'd have a vague sense of the sermon's content, but not much beyond that in terms of specifics or application in our lives.[13]

By contrast, for another sermon it was clear that the presenter had a laser focus on getting a specific point across about holiness. "Today we'll examine a specific strategy for developing holiness: training our minds to dwell more on conversations, habits, activities, and relationships with other people that have as their purpose drawing ourselves and others closer to God." Having that specific focus, communicating it explicitly, and judging

---

12. Robinson, *Biblical Preaching*, 43.

13. In the next section, we will examine the concept of an *advance organizer*. As we will see, an advance organizer is similar to what Long calls "focus and function statements." According to Long, such statements "should be clear, unified, and relatively simple." He notes a similar problem to the one described here when a specific focus and function statement is not presented. "Focus statements like 'God is Love,' 'the birth of Jesus,' or 'God calls us to justice' are too vague to be helpful," *The Witness of Preaching*, 132.

all sermon content against that focus, facilitated a planning process that made the sermon a memorable learning experience.

As another example, I recall still—some 15 years later—a sermon that communicated the main idea that faith is not something that just happens but requires conscious nurturing. That main idea was explicitly communicated at the start and repeated in various ways throughout. At one juncture the main idea was reiterated using a rhetorical question. The speaker asked us to consider what we read and what were the likely effects of the time spent in that reading. The main point relating to faith development was motivated by a simple question that was suggested we might ask about reading choices: "Is reading this book/magazine/newsletter, etc. likely going to help increase my faith?" The speaker assured us that there is surely a place for recreational reading, but even challenging us to ask the question was a helpful way to make more concrete the main idea that Sunday and to help the listeners absorb to the key point of the sermon.

Linking to the Point

As highlighted in the dissertation development scenario described in the preceding section, arriving at a clear, focused, specific point[14] for a sermon can represent the main struggle in sermon development, but arriving at that point drives and facilitates all subsequent preparation decisions. It is this hard first step that makes the rest of the process easier by providing a yardstick for evaluating the alignment of potential sermon content with the main point. Once the point has been explicitly developed, each subsequent development decision should be made with respect to the extent to which it contributes to—or potentially detracts from—the intended main point. Those decisions include answering questions such as:

- What background information or context do listeners need to fully access the point?
- Which listener characteristics will help/hinder getting the point across?

---

14. To avoid unnecessarily cumbersome writing, I will refer going forward to a single focal point driving the preparation of a sermon. However, it should be clear that a sermon might have more than one main point that it is intended to convey. In such circumstances, attention to the principles in this chapter would apply to the development of each of the main points.

- What anecdotes are relevant to the point?
- What examples help illustrate the point?
- To which real-life contexts does the point apply?

Let us reconsider the illustration earlier in this chapter about the bowline knot. Surely, it is of little consequence whether any reader of this book is ever motivated to learn to tie that knot, or even remembers its uses. In deciding to include that example, I explicitly wanted to provide a different context that might help lock in the main point that it is careful preparation—preparation even for the unexpected—on which success hinges. The hiker may not have been rescued except for the hours the Eagle Scout spent learning and practicing the bowline. That sturdy lifeline doesn't "just happen," much as success in delivering an effective sermon that helps listeners gain the intended insights is the result of concerted effort expended in preparation, not something that just happens automatically or naturally.

Subsequent chapters of this book will address some of the questions listed above in greater detail (e.g., the incorporation of humor, fostering application). For now, we'll examine a fourth key principle of sermon preparation—how and why to link sermon content explicitly to the main point. We will begin with some background on how and why presenting listeners with the main point of a sermon—early and often—is effective in helping listeners to remember the point and benefit from the sermon as intended.

A Framework for Learning, Recall, and Application

A researcher in the 1960s, David Ausubel, introduced the concept of an *advance organizer*. Almost from the time he introduced the idea, there were misunderstandings about what Ausubel intended. He often tried to clarify what an advance organizer was . . . and what it wasn't.

According to Ausubel, an advance organizer is relevant introductory material—in any format: verbal, visual, text, graphic—presented at the beginning of instruction for the purpose of transmitting listeners a framework for assimilating the new ideas, facts, concepts, or principles to be learned and used. The research on advance organizers is clear: learning, retention, and usefulness of what is heard are improved when an advance organizer is provided to listeners. Although the discovery of advance organizers came later, Robinson noted the risk of failing to provide listeners with some kind of organizing framework: "While the preacher sees his outline lying before him on the page, only its contents will be heard by the congregation. They do not hear an outline."[15]

A common—and incorrect—way of conceptualizing an advance organizer is found in the trite admonition to "Tell them what you are going to tell them; then tell them, then tell them what you told them." Another common—and incomplete—strategy is to provide the bullet points of a sermon topic or an outline in advance. For example, a priest whose sermons always have a profound impact on us routinely provides an alliterative outline at the beginning of his sermons, along the lines of "Today we will look at three aspects of prayer: the purpose of prayer, the practice of prayer, and the potential of prayer." Although each of these techniques can be helpful, each falls short of what we know about cognitive organization.

It *is* an important aspect of preparation and delivery to literally, carefully, and routinely state what the intended purpose of a sermon is. But an advance organizer is more than a specific topic statement. An effective advance organizer has three characteristics: 1) it is presented at the start of a sermon; 2) it is at a higher level of abstraction and generality; and 3) it provides listeners with an organizing framework that makes it possible for them to integrate the content of the sermon into what they already know.

The cognitive science underlying advance organizers relies on a well-established process involved in learning; namely, that new knowledge, concepts, and principles, and most effectively learned, retained, and used when they are related or linked to specific, relevant concepts, principles, and ideas that already established in our existing cognitive structures. The most effective teaching is that which associates the new learning with existing knowledge. Simply put, it is important to ensure that new learning intended to accrue from a sermon is filed in the "right" place and that the new learning is connected to listeners' previously learned principles and prior experiences so that it is deemed appropriate and easily recalled in future, relevant situations.[16] To explain this further, I'll briefly digress into an introductory look at the cognitive science that underlies advance organizers.

---

15. Robinson, *Biblical Preaching*, 131.

16. A related learning phenomenon has been discovered in the context of the reading comprehension portion of SAT tests. Researchers have found that there is some advantage to test-takers if they actually read the questions first, before reading the passage on which they are based. This is exactly the opposite of what a test-taker would naturally do. However, reading the questions first serves to heighten awareness of what should be attended to when reading the passage with the result of better learning/performance. The linkage to sermons is clear: if listeners know in advance what is going to be most salient in a presentation, they are more likely to learn, retain, and be able to use it.

Are You Ready?

According to those who research how we learn—cognitive scientists—each of us has an existing cognitive structure—a framework, if you will—into which we place new information. We have all structured and organized our knowledge differently. We have created unique cognitive frameworks, but we are all the same in the sense that we incorporate new learning into whatever existing structures we have in place. To have the greatest potential for recall and application in our lives, any new learning must be meaningfully related to what we already know.

An illustration from my bedroom closet may be helpful. If I were to receive a new short-sleeve sport shirt as a birthday gift, I'd likely hang it in that closet. Let's now think of that closet as representing my mind. I already have some shirts, pants, and other items hanging in my closet, and the way I have them organized represents my existing framework. The shirt I just received as a gift represents new information. I *could* hang the new shirt in several different places. If I were to hang it with dress shirts, it might be fairly easy to find when I need to find or want to wear the new shirt. If I were to hang it with winter coats, I may never see it again. I might even "forget" that have it until I serendipitously stumble across it when winter rolls around—a time when it's likely I'd not find it relevant to wear. However, if I were to hang it with other short-sleeve sport shirts, there is a good chance I'd see it when getting dressed on a summer day and I'd be able to consider wearing it when the relevant opportunity arose.

To torturously extend this analogy only slightly further, if I was given the shirt (new learning) with no advice on where to store it, it could end up anywhere—and forever be forgotten. ("Remember that yellow shirt I got you for your birthday a few years ago? How come you never wear it?") On the other hand, if I was given the new shirt *accompanied by guidance* on *how to integrate it* (an advance organizer) into the wardrobe I already own and ideas regarding its use, I'm considerably more likely to appreciate the sermon—um, . . . I mean, shirt.

That's what an advance organizer is: a framework that provides guidance on what the new learning is, how it relates to other things I have learned, and examples of how and when the new learning might be needed and applied. ("I know you already have a few sports shirts, but I thought you'd like this shirt for our vacation trip next month because it has a lot of pockets for things, it takes up only a little room in a suitcase, and it doesn't wrinkle.")

The reason advance organizers are effective is because, as mentioned previously, each of our mental closets are arranged differently—ranging from no apparent system of organization at all, to an elaborate, highly specific, unwavering organizational system.[17] In essence, advance organizers help listeners to connect the main ideas of a sermon with their own, existing cognitive structures and provide guidance on where to "hang" the new information. This helps avoid two obvious, but problematic, strategies that a listener might use for storing the new information. Lacking the guidance of an advance organizer, a listener could file the new information in a relevant but non-optimal location, making retrieval and use difficult. Worse, the information could be linked to a random, unrelated place in his or her cognitive organization which could essentially preclude the information from ever being recalled or having any positive effect in contexts where it would be germane.

For example, a sermon listener could link the main idea of a sermon to a song the choir sang that day—perhaps a song that is only rarely a part of a service, or one that the person especially dislikes. The intended message of the sermon would then have the greatest probability of being recalled and impactful in the person's life only when stimulated for recall by the (rare) occasion of hearing the disliked hymn.

Readers of this chapter have almost certainly had a similar experience that illustrates this phenomenon of the way knowledge, memories, and ideas are linked in our minds:

- opening a musty box in the attic brings to mind a visit to a grandparent's home decades earlier;
- an overflowing bathtub prompts detailed recall of a rafting trip from several years ago;
- the smell of Dove soap calls to mind a fond memory of Mom;
- seeing a vintage automobile elicits memories of a high school prom;
- a friend's remark in conversation surfaces a memory—seemingly out of nowhere—of a favorite childhood television show.

---

17. Personally, I am on the latter end of this closet organizing continuum, perhaps even nearing an OCD organizational style. Others, like me, who can't help but hang their dress shirts, organized by color, with all collars pointing in the same direction can perhaps relate to what I think of a an "optimal organization system."

In summary, an advance organizer does not simply "tell 'em what you are going to tell 'em." Rather, it provides a purposeful framework for integrating the content of the sermon into the existing cognitive organizations of the listeners in a way that makes the information most accessible, useful, and effectual. An advance organizer should be provided at the beginning of a sermon, and it is often most effective if it is referred to at appropriate junctures during the sermon.

With the closet organization as background, what would an advance organizer look like when applied to developing and delivering a sermon? The following paragraphs provide an example—and a non-example—of an advance organizer in the context of sermons. Table 2-2 captures some of the key attributes of what an advance organizer is, and isn't.

> *"Let's think for a moment about some of the job and social relationships we have. Co-workers, neighbors, club members. Relationships are good and necessary, but the social and employment contexts we operate in each day can sometimes present difficult challenges regarding how to align our words and actions with the kind of purity and respect toward others that honors God. Today, I am going to address how to avoid difficult sexual situations in the workplace and other social situations of our daily lives. We will be deriving three Scriptural guidelines for developing and maintaining healthy, holy relationships. And, we'll be learning how to apply the Scriptures on that topic to contexts such as carpools, business trips, parent meetings at school, holiday parties."*

This kind of advance organizer essentially tells us that we will be getting a new shirt and provides a strong suggestion for where to hang it. The preceding is a longer example of an advance organizer, but length is unrelated to the cognitive principle of what the advance organizer is designed to accomplish. I witnessed one preacher incorporating the principle in just a single sentence. In fact, he began the sermon with what he literally called the "Sermon in a Sentence." The expository message that Sunday involved David and some of his experiences recorded in I Samuel 18. The practical theme of the sermon was stated as "Today, I'd like to focus on three key points: When people try to tear you down, you need a friend to fill you up and God to hold you together." Boom. A sermon—an advance organizer—in a sentence. The balance of the sermon described some typical situations in which we might feel torn down by circumstances, events, or people; it suggested practical ways to find and connect with a friend to support us in those times; and it emphasized our need to lean on God as the source of strength for thriving in the midst of such struggles. The sentence served not only to communicate the principle he wanted us to learn, but also as the framework on which we were able to hang those three shirts.

In contrast, the succinct opening, *"This Sunday I'll be talking about Biblical male/female relationships,"* only hints at what the gift will be. Worse, it essentially says, *"You're on your own"* regarding where to hang it. It fails to help listeners have lasting recall of the sermon's content in ways that allow the important concepts presented to be at the ready when relevant.

Table 2-2
Key Attributes of Effective Advance Organizers

Advance Organizers are . . .	*Advance Organizers are Not . . .*
unique for each sermon.	general, the same across all situations or similar for each sermon.
presented at the beginning of a sermon and revisited throughout.	presented only at the beginning of a sermon.
developed "frameworks" that aid listeners in appropriately storing information for later use.	a simple topic statement, summary, main idea, piquing question, or objective of the sermon.
mechanisms to help listeners relate what they already know to what will be presented.	created without first understanding listeners' existing background knowledge of the topic.
ways of helping listeners connect what is to come to their unique, individual, existing knowledge, and experiences.	statements about abstract or de-contextualized purpose, vague overviews.
presented in various modes (e.g., text, verbal, visual).	bulleted lists of each point in a sermon.
most effective when presented explicitly.	effective when listeners must gauge importance, relevance, or application on their own.
a technique for establishing cognitive connections between what is known and what is unknown.	a review of previous topics in sermon series and/or a list of upcoming topics in the series.

Ensuring the Point is the Point

The final aspect of sermon preparation has to do with the nature of language. The longstanding aim of any sermon is surely not simply to put language out there for listeners, but for that language to be clearly understood. It is recorded in Nehemiah "They read from the Book of the Law of God, making it clear and giving the meaning so that the people understood what was being read."[18]

However, fostering meaning and understanding is challenging at least in part because language is so tricky. In my own life, I've witnessed hundreds of examples of how a main idea, word, image, or whole presentation was intended to convey one thing, yet conveyed something completely different than—even opposite of—what was was being attempted. Cognitive scientists refer to these two things as the *nominal* message (that is, the message that is intended to be conveyed) and the *effective* message (that is, the one that viewers or listeners actually take away from the presentation).

My first experience with this—although I lacked the technical vocabulary at the time—was when I noticed my young son, David, watching television. I knew that his room had not yet been cleaned as he was supposed to have done, so I asked: "Dave, why don't you head upstairs and clean up your room now?"

His response? "Because I'm in the middle of this television show." "It's still pretty clean from last week." "No one is really going to see my room if I just keep the door closed." Dave interpreted my question as, well, a question, and he responded with exactly what he interpreted me to be asking for—reasons why he didn't feel like heading upstairs to clean his room. In retrospect, I think that I had some expectation that he would interpret my question *not* as a question, but as a sociolinguistic nicety that obscured what it really was intended to be: a directive. The nominal message was not the effective message. What I had intended to communicate was not what was received.

There are plenty of familiar examples of this kind of nominal/effective message mismatch. To illustrate, I sometimes write the following on the chalkboard for one of my classes:

"I hate visiting relatives."

I then ask my class by a show of hands to indicate who among them interpreted that sentence to mean that they dislike going to visit people

18. Nehemiah 8:8 (NIV)

they are related to. About half of the students raise their hands. I then ask who interpreted it to mean *precisely the opposite*—that is, who doesn't enjoy people coming to visit them—and the other half of the class signals that this was their interpretation.

The same phenomenon applies to the spoken word—the typical medium of sermons—and involves the intonation and emphasis we use. For example, something spoken in monotone and such as, "Joe did not throw the ball to Sue" could be interpreted in substantially different ways if even a single word or two is emphasized over others, as in:

"*Joe* did not throw the ball to Sue." [Meaning: Someone else threw it.]

"Joe *did not* throw the ball to Sue." [Meaning: Denial that Joe was involved.]

"Joe did not *throw* the ball to Sue." [Meaning: He kicked it.]

"Joe did not throw *the ball* to Sue." [Meaning: He threw the racquet.]

"Joe did not throw the ball to *Sue*." [Meaning: He threw it to Nathan.]

Not to let other modes of communication off the hook, it should be noted that this subjectivity of perceptions involving language and potential mismatch between nominal and effective messages is not limited to written text. Cognitive science has discovered that the same uncertainty and potential for miscommunication can occur for visual images as well. For example, most introductory textbooks in psychology present the image shown in Figure 2-5. Is it a young woman? An old woman? Most viewers of the image will "see" one or the other—at least initially—and, with some effort and perhaps cues as to what to look for, they may be able to see the other.[19] Importantly, what one sees in the image is often related to one's own characteristics, with younger viewers tending to see the young woman and older viewers finding the older woman in their first impression.

---

19. According to science writer, Yasemin Saplakoglu, "What You See in This Famous Optical Illusion," the drawing is the creation of a British cartoonist named William Ely Hill, who published it in 1915 with the humorous caption "My Wife and My Mother-in-Law." It depicts both an old woman with her gaze toward the lower left of the frame, and a young woman with her face turned away looking over her right shoulder. If it helps, the old woman's nose is the young woman's chin. The older woman is wearing a fur collared coat; the younger woman wears a thin choker. The older woman's left eye is the younger woman's left ear.

Are You Ready?

Figure 2-5

Subjectivity of Perceptions

What does this subjectivity of perceptions have to do with sermons? To be sure, the fact that we all interpret words or images differently isn't a flaw; it isn't a human characteristic that can or should be corrected; one view or interpretation shouldn't be labeled "right" and another "wrong." Perhaps most importantly for our purposes, any discrepancy between what is intended and what is received isn't the *listener's* problem. Instead, responsibility for any slippage between the nominal message and the effective message rests squarely on the shoulders of the presenter.[20]

As indicated previously, introducing the main intended point of the sermon at its beginning and referencing it often during a sermon are helpful. But repetition of something that was not accurately received as intended will serve only to reinforce any misunderstandings. Rephrasing the main point during the sermon can aid listeners to clarify their initial understandings. Giving listeners opportunities to revise their understanding by stating the main point in different ways throughout the sermon provokes assimilation of the consistent message intended. Finally, when a common misunderstanding is anticipated or feared, it is helpful to simply and explicitly state not only what the main point is, but also *what it is not*.

20. Although cognitive science has not examined how God works in such "slippage" situations, thankfully, the Holy Spirit intervenes!

Sermon Science

All of us who teach have experienced that there are concepts we know listeners will have difficulty processing. In everyday human communication, it is often helpful to invoke the technique of saying what we intend to communicate as well as what we don't. We can imagine this principle operating in a conversation between a husband and wife about their income and financial position. In the following snippet of that conversation, notice how the clarity of the point emerges as the man or woman tries to capture "I want you to understand X [main point]. My point is *not* Z [a potential misunderstanding of the point he or she is trying to get across]. Again, I am saying X [main point rephrased, expanded, paraphrased]."

> *"Dear, I've got to tell you that I'm getting really weary of what I've been doing in my career for the last several years. I just don't think I can continue this way."* [Main Point X] . . .

> *"Don't worry: I'm not saying I'm going to do anything rash like quit my job tomorrow and leave us hanging."* [Not Z] . . . *I'm just saying that I think I need to step back and maybe talk to someone about options for my career. I don't know, maybe I need to get involved in something outside of my job that is more fulfilling than what I do every day. I only know that I'm not happy with where things stand, and I need to do something."* [Rephrased Main Point X].

Let's now apply that to sermons. At the risk of a foray into some (for me) poorly known theology, it would seem essential for a minister to state clearly the key idea that he or she would like the congregation to take away from a sermon on predestination. I'll not wade into a precise example of what that specific main point might be but, in the example that follows, I will illustrate this principle by identifying a likely risk in addressing doctrine on predestination. After stating the explicit point of the sermon, it will almost certainly help listeners if an equally explicit companion statement is provided:

> *"Now that we have the main idea in mind that I will be pursuing today regarding predestination, let me clarify some critical things that I am* not *saying. As important as it is to understand the doctrine of predestination, it is equally important to make clear three potential misunderstandings. First, I am* not *saying that predestination cancels out the possibility of any one of us freely choosing to follow Jesus—or choosing not to. Second, I'm* not *saying that predestination voids the gift of free will God has given us. Third, I'm* not *saying we are merely marionettes of a great puppet master. As we will see, the doctrine of predestination and free will are not in conflict and we will look at examples of each feature of our faith."*

In short, just as it is important for listeners to gain an understanding of the main point that is intended in a sermon by explicitly laying out that main point, it is often important to head off potential misunderstandings by explicitly confronting potential or likely misunderstandings. Whereas ensuring that the main point is received by listeners is essential for all sermons, actively heading off potential misunderstandings may not be routinely necessary. The main point of the sermon and the speaker's experience with the extent to which that point evokes potential misunderstandings provide guidance as to when it will be helpful to make "I'm *not saying* Z" as explicit as what *is* being said about X.

CONCLUSIONS

This chapter addressed some key prerequisites that underlie sermon preparation. First, it is essential to consider the characteristics of the listeners. A sermon that might prompt real awareness, insights, and changes in the spiritual lives for one group might entirely fail to reach others.

Second, we examined ideas for—and the benefits of—developing, incorporating, and sustaining focus on an intended aim for a sermon. It is recommended that the main point of a sermon be crafted in explicit, written form in the course of developing a sermon. The struggle of arriving at a sharpened point for a sermon is rewarded by the guidance that it subsequently provides regarding what to include, highlight, illustrate, and elaborate upon in the sermon itself.

Third, sermons should be developed with attention to helping listeners to appropriately organize and store what they are hearing but also to providing them with a framework—an advance organizer to aid in processing, incorporating, remembering, and using the learning that is intended.

Finally, and foreshadowing the upcoming chapters that more explicitly incorporate some of what we know about designing instruction, I will differentiate between two terms that I have used somewhat synonymously. In this chapter, I've frequently used the term *listeners* to describe members of a congregation in attendance for a sermon, members of a Bible study, or children in a Sunday school class. Perhaps just as frequently, I've used the term *learners*. There is a slight—but significant—difference. Clearly it is desirable for those who hear a sermon to be active listeners. However, it is equally clear that sermons are not meant solely to be heard, but to instruct—to result in meaningful changes in the lives of the listeners—and that should be the primary aim of a sermon. To that end, in the following chapters, the focus similarly sharpens to crafting sermons with the best hope of effecting those changes.

CHAPTER 3

The Lectern and the Pulpit

Many of the learning principles covered in the previous chapter were developed at a time when a lecture was the primary mode for teaching. Although the lecture format is still often appropriate, useful, and widely used, it is important to be clear that a sermon is not a lecture.

A lecture and a sermon might have in common the goal of promoting learning and affecting real changes in the knowledge, skills, perspectives, or lives of the listeners, but there are key differences. Over the past several decades, the traditional lecture format is observed less and less often in college classrooms and in church sanctuaries. Most likely, this is because research on learning has discovered and repeatedly demonstrated across diverse contexts that maximum learning and change occurs when listeners are more actively engaged in the interaction and not merely passive attendees.

In contemporary churches, the current reality across diverse denominations is that few sermons are highly interactive; sermons rarely provide opportunities for listeners to engage as full participants. This observation is not a critique, just the state of affairs. The current reality is to some extent an artifact of various religious traditions and there are often good reasons for those traditions that are beyond the scope of this book.

On the other hand, it is clear that the leadership in some churches recognizes and values active engagement in learning and spiritual growth. I suspect that this in at least some measure accounts for the fact that, increasingly, churches provide distinct opportunities for more interactive engagement via sponsorship of home Bible study groups, "life groups," or other mechanisms for subgroups from a congregation to review, extend, and inquire about key points in a sermon or explore applications.

Nonetheless, for purposes of this chapter, I have assumed a contemporary norm for the format of a sermon. That norm has some resemblances to a lecture. For one, a sermon is typically an event consisting nearly exclusively of an oral presentation by a congregational minister, pastor, priest, or teacher. For another, sermons typically have a specific topic or intended objective in mind, as well as a constrained time frame for delivery.

Because there exist some commonalities, there are aspects of sermons that are similar enough to lectures so as to benefit from attention to what can make a lecture an effective learning event for its listeners. However, beyond examining adaptations of the lecture mode of presentation that are helpful for preparing and delivering a sermon, this chapter examines some important distinctions and critical mistakes that are made when delivering a lecture that should also be avoided when delivering a sermon.

A SERMON IS NOT A LECTURE

Although there are some surface similarities between a lecture and a sermon, there are also important differences. The lecture format is appropriate given its modest goal: to simply convey information. However, even in large college-level courses where lectures are appropriate, a lecture should not merely convey information that a student can readily access in some other way. For example, it would be an inappropriate use of the lecture format—and an inefficient use of class time—if a lecturer simply restated information that was available for students to read in the assigned textbook for the course.

Perhaps as many readers can affirm, many garden-variety lectures are often just plain boring. As Thomas Long has observed in his book on preaching, sermons can also sometimes (regrettably) be characterized that way. "We have to admit, of course, that many sermons are boring, incompetent, or faithless. Jesus, the living Word, was crucified, and the preached Word can be crucified too."[1]

In describing sermons as the learning events, in preceding chapters I've invoked principles of instructional design. In subsequent chapters, I'll continue to show how many of those principles are relevant to lectures and sermons. However, it's also important to recognize that the context of offering spiritual direction, knowledge, insights or applications differs in important ways from delivering a lecture.

1. Long, *The Witness of Preaching*, 17.

College freshman may endure a lecture read from an aging professor's yellowed paper notes to an audience of 500 students in an Introduction to Economics course. In such cases, they are likely to do so because it is a mandated course and passing ECON101 is required for graduation. By contrast, attending sermons is optional. There are no participation points awarded for sermons. There isn't a test. The textbook doesn't change from year to year. Congregants aren't evaluated. Although understanding the key point of a sermon might be relevant to our "eternal graduation," it is worth keeping in mind that attendance isn't mandatory and may not factor into our final grade!

READING AND RETELLING

Whereas a student might feel powerless and acquiesce in the face of a lecture read aloud from an instructor's well-rehearsed written script, a sermon should never simply be read to a congregation. Again, quoting Long:

> "A 'written sermon' is a contradiction in terms. Of course, many sermons are written down before they are preached, but a sermon itself occurs not in the writing but in the preaching. A sermon, by definition, is a spoken event. This distinction is important, because speaking and writing are not merely two separate but equal channels of communication. The effects of the spoken word are markedly different from those of the written word."[2]

Not only does an engaging, oral presentation of a sermon (versus reading one) carry differential impact due to the power of the spoken word, but it is also a callous matter of efficiency. Of what advantage would it be to listeners to actually attend a church service to hear a sermon read aloud if they could simply read a sermon transcript for themselves at a convenient time?[3] In fact, in some respects, it would a greater benefit to congregants if they could read a written sermon than to have it read to them because the listener's access and retention would not be limited to the temporal dimension of the reading. Indeed, if congregants were able to simply read a

---

2. Long, *The Witness of Preaching*, 262.

3. I am of course not taking into account here of the value of fellowship with other believers, congregational worship, and other common aspects of church gatherings. Strictly from an efficiency perspective when considering additional travel time, costs, and logistical challenges of coming to/from a church service, the remotely accessed sermon wins hands down.

sermon for themselves instead of having a sermon read to them, they could take whatever time they deemed necessary to read, process, contemplate certain ideas, re-read or review critical points, look up unknown words or expressions, and so on.

A cousin to the practice of reading a sermon script is the retelling of a Scripture reading. It is common in many faith traditions for an extended passage of Scripture to form the foundation or key text for a sermon. This can be helpful as a runway for launching a sermon; it should not be the entire flight.

The retelling mistake frequently occurs in sermons involving parables. After all, parables are engaging stories. Stories are powerful, memorable, and can function to cement common bonds. At my own family gatherings, we often come together and retell stories involving childhood recollections, memorable family events, quirky family members, embellished past accomplishments and other oft-repeated narratives. As an adult—just like my children did when they were younger and being prepared for bedtime—I love to hear a favorite story and I can listen with rapt attention to nearly any variation of it.

In church contexts, a sermon based on the parable of the prodigal son is a commonly encountered variation on the theme of reading a sermon. After presenting the key text from the gospel of Luke, the speaker then provides the same chronology but with elaborations about the wealthy father's two sons. Some details are added about one son who requests an early distribution from his father's estate, spurns his family, and squanders that inheritance. Description of the other son who is faithful and obedient to his father (albeit resentful of his brother) comprises some elaboration regarding the time- and funding-limited fun had by the prodigal son, his end state when the funds run out, and the decision process of the prodigal son in concluding that he was better off in his pre-prodigal days. The final part of the retelling involves an elaborated description of the prodigal's journey home, the father's joy and celebration at his return, and the brother's jealous reaction.

If your reaction to the preceding summary of the parable was along the lines of "Yeah, yeah. I've heard all that; get on with the point you are trying to make here," then your reaction is not far from that of many listeners to such retellings who tacitly ask during the sermon: "Hey. Wait a minute. Didn't we just hear this story moments ago?"

My own recollection of hearing the prodigal son story retold as a sermon was the great detail provided regarding to the wayward son's diet. In describing the famine that came over the land and the dire situation the son found himself in, I recall the speaker dwelling on what constituted the feed that would have been provided for pigs at the time. I am confident that memory is *not* what the pastor had hoped I'd take away from the sermon, but that is always a concern with a simple retelling. As we saw in the previous chapter, lack of a crisp focus on a central main take-away can stunt listeners understanding and growth. A simple retelling that substitutes interesting details can do the same.

Simple retellings rival scripted sermon readings in their inefficiency. Perhaps most regrettably, they may not add much more to learning or spiritual insights than the original story in its original form. Simply reading a sermon or retelling a key text both fall short in terms of their potential to help listeners lock in, recall, and apply the intended lessons to their lives. The most undesirable outcome is also possible; namely, that reading or retelling will cause listeners to recall only conjectures or marginal details about the story, or to tune out altogether.

PHILOLOGY: WHATEVER *THAT* IS!

In the previous chapter, I described a key idea for aiding listeners to attend to the intended main idea and key points of a sermon so that they would most likely be available for recall and application in later life situations when they would be relevant. In doing so, I described a technical idea, the *advance organizer*, because that term captures the whole of what I intended convey. Purposefully, I quickly pivoted to more commonly encountered terminology to illustrate how an advance organizer works, and readers may recall the analogy that was provided regarding being given the gift of a shirt along with information on where the shirt should be hung to make it easy to find and wear in appropriate situations. That pivot meant that I did not invoke a host of other technical language that would ordinarily be encountered when considering advance organizers such as *cognitive processing, rehearsal, schema, zones of proximal development, subsumption, mnemonic devices*, and dozens of others.

Why did I purposefully avoid complicating the main idea that I was attempting to convey about advance organizers with those other concepts? Because they didn't matter at that juncture!

To clarify, it's not that those other concepts don't matter *at all*, it's just that familiarity with those concepts wasn't necessary to convey the main idea regarding sermon organization. In my judgment as a writer, I concluded that readers would not need to be exposed to those concepts in order grasp the main point I was trying to communicate about having, focusing on, and providing a mechanism for listeners to grasp and retain a main point. A concern I had in writing about advance organizers was that if I invoked additional academic concepts that weren't central to my intended main point, I could actually detract from my intended goal.

I had two specific worries. First, I was worried that other, unnecessary technical jargon might be simply glossed over by the reader, thus having no effect and simply being a waste of the reader's time. My other worry was of greater concern. I feared that invoking any of those other technical concepts could introduce unnecessary confusion and that those non-central concepts might cause readers to disengage from the topic or actually detract from their understanding about the main point I was working to build.

I imagine that many readers are now asking themselves: "So what does all of that have to do with the curious heading of this section regarding philology?" Thanks for bearing with me.

As promised, it is something that I have purposed to do only rarely, but I am venturing into one of the (many) areas that is not a core expertise of mine because the concept of *philology* is relevant at this juncture. I suspect that the term may be unfamiliar to some readers. For many other readers, this technical concept was likely encountered as a part of a divinity degree program, seminary training, or other formal coursework in preparation for pastoral ministry. My rudimentary understanding is that philology is concerned with the study of human language as it is used in oral or written form. Although such studies can involve comparative analyses of contemporary language, philological excursions can be useful for developing a sermon to the extent that they provide insights on the historical roots of written or oral language—that is, on the origins, meanings, and usages of words, phrases, idioms and the like—from sources in the distant past.

The main point of this section is to prompt consideration of the following questions when preparing or delivering a sermon:

"Is delving into ancient languages essential for my listeners to grasp, recall, and apply the main intended point(s) of this sermon?" or

"Will such a foray into the historical roots be more of a distraction—and perhaps even a hindrance—to the main goal?"

Let us return for a moment to a key takeaway from Chapter 2 that stressed the importance of knowing one's audience. If one's audience were fellow Classics scholars, comparative linguists, or pastors, delving into philology might be relevant. It might be germane to the scholarly training of seminarians. It might even be relevant if an aspect of the historical roots of a word or expression were salient vis à vis a word or phrase encountered in the modern language spoken by the intended audience for a sermon. Most of the time, it's none of these.

As an example of this, I believe that, to this day, a sermon I heard in the past gave me a serviceable comprehension of a concept, transliterated from the Greek word, κοινωνία. My understanding is that the word connotes "fellowship" or "sense of Christian community among believers." I never regretted being exposed to philological background on the term *koinonia*; I am somewhat proud that I was able to recall it decades later for the purpose of including it here.

On the other hand, I don't believe in the 35 or so years since I heard the sermon that delved into that term and its origins that I have ever actually used or needed to refer to it. Most importantly, I am somewhat dismayed that, although I retained some memory of a single Greek vocabulary word, I didn't retain whatever the main point of that sermon was. I'm fairly confident that the preacher who gave that sermon would be equally dismayed at my failure to retain the main point from that Sunday.

At a micro level—and I realize that this may border on heresy to some readers—I would argue that each temptation to invoke a Greek, Aramaic, or other ancient language in a sermon be held up against a criterion of need. Again, considering listeners as learners, the following questions are relevant to introducing an unknown word that might actually be a distraction:

"Is it necessary for listeners to understand the origin or meaning of this term?"

"Will probing the philological aspects of this term foster—or distract from—the essential point I am trying to convey in this sermon?"

Sometimes, the answer to one of these questions is a confident "Yes." There may be times when it is judged to be of some benefit; there may even be times when, in the development of a sermon, such an excursion is essential. The key point of this section is *not* that all philological explications should be avoided. The key idea is that, even when judged to be essential, it is imperative to explicitly consider the cost/benefit ratio of its inclusion regarding readers' grasp of the main intended point. Would, for example, the time spent introducing a Greek term and its roots be more efficaciously allocated to the inclusion of an additional illustration of how the main idea can be put into real-life practice? How does the philological path aid listeners in their understanding of the main point? How does the digression help cement learning of the main idea? Will waxing philological help or hinder listeners' grasp of the focal point? A simple answer to all of these questions is "When in doubt, leave it out."

MAKING MEANING ACCESSIBLE

In the same vein as the importance of evaluating whether an unfamiliar word or concept from an ancient language will promote or detract from listeners' attention to the intended point of a sermon, a more general recommendation is that *all* language, illustrations, and examples used in a sermon should be measured against their accessibility. It is certain that a homilist would want everyone listening to a sermon to find meaning and application to their lives. Sometimes, however, what is included may not support that goal. Careful examination *a priori* of some aspects of even contemporary language—especially, as we will see, what might be called "church language"—is critical.

One way to help gauge the extent to which a term, phrase, or concept will be accessible to all listeners is to consider a helpful three-category way that language experts use to classify our vocabularies. A first bucket for sorting vocabulary is called the "Expressive" category. A person's expressive vocabulary storehouse contains all the words that he or she readily uses in spoken language. We fully understand and freely use these words.

A second bucket is called our "Receptive" vocabulary, or words that we understand when we hear them. These are words that wouldn't readily come to mind in a conversation or that we don't ordinarily use in speaking to others. We still comprehend what is meant by these words; we just don't typically use them ourselves when we communicate with others.

It is perhaps easiest to think of expressive vocabulary as our reservoir of words for speaking and receptive vocabulary as our reservoir of words for hearing. Our receptive vocabulary storehouses are much larger than our expressive vocabularies; our expressive language is just a subset of our receptive language. We can understand a lot more than we typically use. As an example, a friend might say to me: "That was quite a kerfuffle at the budget meeting today over the purchase of new choir robes!" I know he means that there was a ruckus, an animated disagreement, a dust-up, a row, because *kerfuffle* is part of my receptive vocabulary. However, if I had been the one telling my friend about the budget meeting, it never would have occurred to me to describe it as a kerfuffle because that's simply not a term in my expressive storehouse. I would have had to use a word that *was* in my expressive vocabulary, such as "stir," or "commotion," or "fuss," or even "brouhaha"!

The third vocabulary category is the easiest to explain: it's the bucket that contains all other words not in our expressive or receptive storehouses. It comprises the words we neither use nor understand their meaning when we hear them. For me—and perhaps all of us—this category is probably the largest. As I flipped through a modern dictionary, I was humbled by the vast quantity of words that were unfamiliar to me—*anodyne, felicitate, insouciance, limn, megillah, miasma, organoleptic, perdure, prothalamion, sere, turbid*—that were nonetheless apparently current and judged worthy of inclusion in a contemporary dictionary. For me, the preceding list could go on and on; it would include far more words than are in my expressive or receptive vocabularies combined! Indeed, I listed as examples only non-technical terms. If I had included technical terms from geometry, physics, engineering, medicine, visual arts, automotive mechanics, aeronautics, information technology, marine biology, accounting, cosmetology (and, yes, theology) or hundreds of other domains and professions with their own technical languages, my receptive and expressive assets would be miniscule in comparison.

A whole other constellation of words that may not be in listeners' receptive or expressive vocabularies aren't technical, obscure, or arcane. Many times I've *heard* the term "Gen Xer" to describe someone from a recent generation but—I'll admit it—I don't have an immediate grasp of the meaning of that term and typically end up having to (re)Google it. Slang expressions fall into this same category. A Gen Xer would readily understand what was intended if a friend said he was so *jelly* that she scored tickets to a concert. The first time I heard someone's claimed needs described disparagingly as *bougie*, I had some sense from context that it might be related to *bourgeois*, but I kept quiet and looked it up later.

In short, for all of us, the volume of words falling outside our expressive or receptive vocabulary vessel is vast, and the implications for creating and delivering sermons from which listeners can learn the intended main ideas are clear. A grossly oversimplified but reasonable summary of the primary implication might be along the lines of: "Use words people will understand." However, similar to other recommendations contained in this book that may seem obvious on first blush, the admonition that caution be used in choosing words and expressions for sermons bears deeper examination.

One particular way that sermons can be unintentionally inaccessible involves the use of language that is particular to the domain of a religious tradition. Some years ago, when I was speaking to a colleague at work about an important spiritual topic, I found myself using words that I'm pretty sure he didn't understand. Maybe I referred to the *homily* I'd heard on Sunday or the *home fellowship* we were starting. I don't recall exactly what brought the problem to my attention: it may have been the quizzical look on his face or the absence of any follow-up questions. The technical way of describing that communication failure is that the words I chose to use were in my expressive vocabulary but were not in his receptive vocabulary. The less flattering way of characterizing my interaction was that I was using jargon that was exclusive to those in a club in which he was not a member—and my word choices clearly signaled to him that he wasn't.

It is important for me to take responsibility on this point: it was *not* his comprehension problem; it was *my* communication problem.

Since that time, I have become even more acutely aware of the extent to which our language is non-inclusive, perhaps particularly in sermons. By this, I don't intend to invoke modern day concerns about pronoun usage, gender identities, or other contemporary controversies. I also don't believe it's ever purposeful. I do, however, think it's important to recognize that sermons can include jargon that is not accessible to "outsiders," and which unintentionally can make them feel that way. In cognitive science terms, we can incorrectly assume that all listeners have the same receptive vocabulary storehouses.

I've started keeping an informal cataloging of insider language with substantial potential to be unfamiliar or possibly seriously misunderstood in church settings. A short, illustrative list of such insider language is shown in Table 3-1 and is intended only to provide some potentially familiar examples. In creating the list, I have purposefully tried to highlight that needlessly difficult-to-access jargon is not unique to high- or low-church contexts.

Table 3-1
Sermon Jargon

What is said...	What it means...
"We're dealing with some *spiritual milk* here."	"Some of the things I'm talking about are really foundational aspects of a new life as a Christian."
"There will be a time of *corporate* prayer on Wednesday evening."	"Everyone is invited to join in a time of prayer on Wednesday evening."
"Please take your Bibles and join me as we *break open the Word*."	"Please open your Bibles and join me in reading some of it."
"I am excited to tell you about the progress of our *church plant* in Collegeville."	"I am excited to tell you about the progress we've made in starting a new church in Collegeville.
"Your *tithes* are really important to our ability to *reach the lost*."	"The money you give helps us to tell others about the good news of Jesus' love for them."
"We believe that Jesus is *consubstantial* with his Father."	"We believe that Jesus and the Father are both of the same essence, both being fully God."
"As you *walk with Jesus* each day..."	"In your daily life as a Christian..."
"Next week, we will be hosting several events related to our *paschal* celebration."	"Next week, we will be hosting several events related to our celebration of Easter/the resurrection."
"There will be *elders* available to pray with you in the narthex at the conclusion of our service if you have anything to *bring before the throne*."	"Some faithful church members will be available to pray with you in the lobby at the back of the church if you have any needs."
"This is our necessary and humble *oblation*."	"This is something that we do as an act of devotion and sacrifice to God."
"After the *benediction*, the *service ministers* will be taking up a *love offering* for our guest speaker."	"We will be leaving time for people to give money in support of our speaker at the end of the service after I ask God for His blessing on us."
"Although our choir doesn't wear *ecclesiastical* garb, I think you will find their performance today to be a *high church* experience.	"Although the choir members aren't dressed in the kind of formal robes that are often seen in Christian churches, their performance will be solemn and rooted in historical tradition."

The entries in the table are drawn from my own sermon experiences. Some readers are likely to find entries on my list that would be familiar receptive language in their congregations; other readers will surely be able to list additional entries that come to mind as potentially inaccessible jargon. In fact, the last few rows of the table are left purposefully blank to stimulate reflection on examples that may be unique to a local context and might warrant consideration. Pausing to reflect on and list a few examples of language outside a sermon listener's receptive vocabulary might be a worthwhile activity.

To put a sharper point on the need to consider accessibility of language to *all* sermon listeners, let us assume for a moment that, for a given sermon, 90% of listeners will be familiar with the terms and concepts being invoked. Typically, that 90% is most likely to be established believers, immersed in a specific faith tradition, or long-time attendees of a given church. However, it is important to be clear about who a sermon is intended to reach. We must ask (and—spoiler alert—my answers to these questions would be, "Certainly not!"): "Is it acceptable that 90% are able to grasp what is being communicated?" "Should the main point of the sermon only be accessible to seasoned parishioners?"

In a typical college lecture, a confused student can at least raise his or her hand and ask for clarification. I don't think I've ever taught a class session when a student didn't ask me to explain what was meant by some technical term or to give another example of an unfamiliar concept I'd just introduced. Those occasions suggest that confusions or inaccurate understandings are routinely present, and they provide an opportunity to promote accurate learning. Conversely, hands are rarely if ever raised to ask for a clarification or an additional example during a sermon. I'm not arguing that there's anything wrong with these traditions. However, I'd also wager that this doesn't mean that all sermons are marked by perfect clarity and homogenous understanding. The main point is that, in the end, it seems better to avoid jargon than to let misunderstandings incubate.

The risk of misunderstandings due to insider language has pervasive implications. Some readers will remember a federal education law passed several years ago called the "No Child Left Behind Act." I found the name of the legislation to be intriguing. I imagine it must have been quite a struggle to come up with that ambitious, promising title for legislation the required all states to develop lists of challenging content to be taught at each grade level and required states to administer tests to measure the extent to which students had learned that content.

Whoever came up with "No Child Left Behind" was surely aware that at least *some* children would fail to measure up to its high expectations for student achievement in American schools—whether due to effort, motivation, instructional quality, parental support, cognitive disabilities, language limitations, or a host of other factors, and regardless of how well funded any educational policies might have been. The logical but unthinkable alternative to naming a law that claimed that no child would be left behind, would be one that recognized almost certainly *some* children would be left behind. However, legislators and the public would never have embraced a law called "Some Children Left Behind" or "Just a Few Children Left Behind." Clearly, the focus for educators *should* be on leaving no one behind, excluding no student from the chance to benefit from a sound learning experience. How much more so should spiritual lessons be targeted to leave no listener behind!

The ability to use context to discern what is meant by an unfamiliar term is a fundamental literacy skill possessed by most adults. For example, anyone unfamiliar with the word *kerfuffle* would most likely understand from context that there must have been a disagreement when the finance committee debated an expenditure for new choir robes. I don't intend here to underestimate the ability of sermon listeners to extract meaning from context when an occasional unfamiliar term is used. However, I'd add two caveats. First, if it were possible to ensure that *all* listeners would be able to readily grasp the main points of a sermon without having to infer meaning from context, wouldn't that be a good thing? Second—and I am not aware of specific research on this topic—I suspect that the jargon-density quotient (JDQ) of a sermon can become of such magnitude that the contextual clues are not helpful. The inferential task becomes too burdensome, and some intended meaning cannot be grasped by those we are trying to reach. When the JDQ reaches some critical level, listening stops and cell phones are checked for time of day and text messages.

I am aware that I am not the first person to make this observation about jargon and to urge caution about the JDQ. The concern has been expressed via clever metaphor by J. R. Briggs:

> "For church outsiders, our worship gatherings can be like watching a foreign film without subtitles. Our insider language confuses those who aren't the regulars, and when people are confused, they tune out."[4]

---

4. Briggs, *Eliminate Christian Jargon from Your Church*, 19.

RESPECTING PERSONS . . . AND THEIR TIME

I'm not saying this is good or bad, but simply observing that we live in a time when every minute is precious. We work to keep our workday from taking time from family life. We struggle to find a few minutes to exercise. We get up earlier, eat faster food, "run" to the store, and communicate with ever shorter text messages (LMK, K?). Time seems more and more to be a precious commodity that we just can't get enough of. At a time when the hectic hustle of my own life was apparently obvious to everyone but me, I recall my Mom expressing her concern for my health with one of those classic Mom observations: "Greg, you are burning the candle at both ends!" At the time, I thought my response was pretty clever: "OK, so where do I get some more wax?" Only much later in life did I realize that I really needed to be a better manager of the wax I'd been given.

Of course, I'm not the only one of us that struggles with making enough time for everything that we'd like to fit in. This is not a book on establishing and maintaining appropriate priorities. On Sunday mornings, it takes a typical family a *lot* of time to get young children—and themselves—dressed, fed, presentable, and transported to church. It is somewhat understandable that church attendance is lagging in the Millennial and Gen Z demographics and that, in the era of Covid-19 concerns, many faithful churchgoers have found viewing a streaming service at home to be a time-saver. For purposes here, it's not my intention to delve into any of those complex issues. I'll only point out that, among all the competing demands and challenges of contemporary life, the decision to allocate time to attend church and to listen to a sermon reflects something that listeners have made a priority in their lives given all of the other ways that time could have been spent.

Accordingly, the main point of this section is to encourage recognition of the preciousness of time when preparing and delivering a sermon. I will invoke another childhood memory at this juncture. This time, it involves one of those sayings that a father uses over and over in one's adolescence and which, years later, continues to direct our perspectives and actions. In my case, it was something my dad was trying to teach about the value of time. Like my Dad, I suppose many parents try to instill the importance of being on time. Commonly, the character quality of being on time is stressed as a good characteristic for the person, himself or herself, to possess.

My Dad approached it from a different angle. He believed that we should not be so much concerned with ourselves, but with how our actions affected others. In his view, being late showed disrespect *for the other person*. He noted that the other person likely had other—perhaps more important—things to do, and he or she would be cheated out of valuable time to attend to those matters if I was late. Being late did not respect the value of *their* time. Accordingly, he encouraged us always to be early, so as not to make another person have to wait for us. His oft-repeated dad-ism based on that principle has been irreversibly imprinted on me: "If you're not 5 minutes early, you're late."

In my role as a university instructor, I have tried to reflect this respect for others' time in my own teaching. I try to start each class on time and end promptly. I try to hold up each contemplated class activity and ask, "Will X be a good use of my students' time in class today?" As teachers, we all have a limited amount of wax to burn; we should want all of it to be as illuminating as possible.

Applied to sermons, it seems respectful to consider how time will be used and to ask a variation of the same question: "Will X be a good use of my listeners' time today?" In subsequent chapters, we'll look at factors to consider when considering the incorporation of stories, jokes, examples, and other elements that can take up considerable chunks of time. The time allocated for those and their corresponding potential for great benefit to listeners suggest that they warrant special attention. To conclude this chapter, however, we will look at a sermon variation of "the three Rs"—Reading, Repeating, and Replaying. These three smaller elements, often incorporated in lectures and sermon contexts, can chip away at available time in smaller increments with little learning benefit.

Reading

An earlier portion of this chapter addressed the undesirability of reading a sermon to listeners. A corollary caution applies to allocating time for listeners to read something themselves or reading it for them. In many cases, a decision about whether something should be read as part of a sermon can boil down to a matter of wise use of time. In other cases, the impulse to ask a congregation to read something might hint at an altogether different concern.

Let's look at a familiar scenario involving a contemporary sermon that incorporates projected text. As a part of one such presentation, imagine that the slide shown in Figure 3-1 with a Scripture from I John 4:20 is projected on the large screens at the front corners of the sanctuary or meeting room.

Figure 3-1

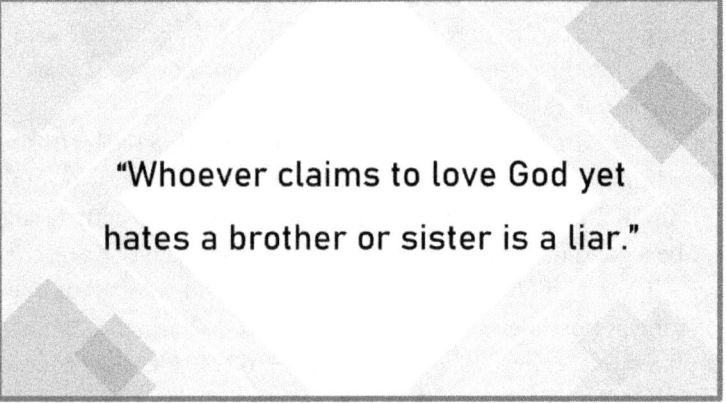

Sample Projected Text

In nearly all adult congregations the simple language of that slide can be easily read in about two seconds. But let's consider three options: Should a speaker simply show the slide and move along? Should the speaker read the words on the slide aloud to the congregation? Should the speaker pause and afford time for the congregation to read that sentence?

Here are three things to consider. First, efficiency. Almost as instantaneous as the mouse click to project the slide, it is likely that persons able to read will have processed it. There may be no need to take the time to re-read it to them.

Second: diversity. When allowing time for congregants to read some projected words, an understandable and sensitive practice is to allow more than enough time for congregants to read the slide. A pause is taken to be certain that everyone in attendance has had ample time to read the verse, point, or other projected text. However, affording a small amount of time for congregants to read the text for themselves is almost never the correct amount of time for the majority of them. A short pause before moving on won't allow some to finish reading; a longer pause can induce boredom and loss of attention for those who finish reading quickly.

A third consideration is cumulative effect. As indicated early on, the purpose of this book is not to provide "rules of thumb" or specific tricks and tips for sermons, but general principles to be considered. In that vein, let's imagine a short pause of 15 seconds afforded a congregation to read some brief textual material on a slide. Adopting that practice for just four such slides has now consumed one of the 37 minutes in an average sermon. Eight slides: two minutes, and so on. Not only is sermon time diminished, but a listener's attention can be also. Too much down time can induce listeners to drift away from the main point of the sermon and toward an email that she needs to send on Monday, the outdoor game his children would like to play that afternoon, the grocery list, or the visit they'll be making to an elderly relative later that day.

Finally, other circumstances are necessary to consider when deciding to read aloud something that has already been presented such as the Scripture shown in Figure 3-1. For example, an awareness and sensitivity to listener characteristics might suggest that it would be helpful to read aloud what some attendees may not find visually accessible; it might both aid and show respect for persons with visual impairments, viewers seated at a distance from the screen, literacy barriers, or other concerns. Of course, the decision to read the text orally may also be deemed important for emphasizing a specific aspect of the projected text.

Repeating

The value of repetition has long been acknowledged as a key to learning. For example, as early as 1924, H. B. Reed referred to repetition as "the golden rule of learning."[5] In 1957, social psychologist Irvin Rock labeled repetition "essential in associative learning."[6] Into the 2000s, then Dean of the University of Virginia School of Business noted repetition as "the first principle of all learning."[7] These affirmations may be only somewhat hyperbolic; the consensus in the field of learning sciences unquestionably affirms that repetition is often a necessary aspect of learning.

There are times when not only reading something, but re-reading or repeating is desirable. A point made in several different ways, said the same way, or just simply repeated over and over can help with recall of an important detail. Application of this key learning principle is ubiquitous in modern advertising: Have any of us escaped television or radio advertisements where the company's telephone number is repeated three times at

5. Reed, "Repetition and Association in Learning," 147.
6. Rock, "The Role of Repetition in Associative Learning," 186.
7. Bruner, "Repetition is the First Principle of All Learning," 1.

the end? "Call 800-555-1116 to get more information. Call now: 800-555-1116. Remember, that number is 800-555-1116."

The same principle applies to repeating information presented in a sermon. As a part of the sermon addressing the verse shown in Figure 3-1, an intended purpose may be that congregants memorize 1 John 4:20. Repeating it several times or, as is sometime done, leading an oral, congregational rehearsal, may be time well spent.

On the other hand, much like the repeated use of "uh" I discovered when listening to the audio tape of my own teaching, repetition can sometimes be a nervous tic, bad habit, or time filler. Like the repeated phone number in the infomercial, repetition can be just plain irritating to listeners. If not reserved for junctures when, purposefully for impact, it is deemed necessary given the intended main point of a sermon (as in the case of Scripture memorization), what might otherwise be a harmless habit can actually become a distraction, impede recall, or prompt listeners to disengage.

In its most benign consequence, needless repetition can simply take up time that might better be allocated to additional concrete examples, pauses for reflection, or other activities that would provide support for accessing the main point of a sermon. The question to be answered here—and it is not one for which a definitive answer is possible because it is dependent on context and purpose—is this: "Is the repetition necessary to support the intended point of the sermon, or is it a habit, a custom?" To answer this question, the technique must be subject to scrutiny for relevance and necessity each time it is invoked.

Replaying

Key ideas in the preceding sections have centered on respecting persons and maximizing the use of time available for a sermon. Teachers in diverse settings can contemplate and apply the ideas presented up to this point to increase efficiency and efficacy. The concerns addressed and suggestions offered might be labeled as "equal opportunity" ideas; they have a sound basis in instructional design, and they apply in a fairly uniform way across nearly all speakers and listeners.

To some extent, however, the previously addressed considerations can be viewed as more technical concerns compared to the idea that will be explored in this section. In the few paragraphs that follow, I'll cautiously attempt to make a delicate third point about time usage in sermons that I realize may not be generalizable or affect all listeners in the same way. I am unaware of any grounding in research on this point, and consensus principles of instructional design are silent on spiritual aspects of learning such as this one.

The topic addressed here arises at the conclusion of a sermon. More precisely, it involves what is often referred to as a closing prayer, led by the speaker who just concluded the sermon or another prayer leader.

First, a caveat: like sermons, I don't advocate formulaic approaches to prayer. The relationships that prayer leaders have with our God are surely unique. I have prayed in agreement with diverse forms of closing prayers on thousands of occasions. In some contexts, the prayer is a tradition-specific benediction, a closing prayer of thankfulness or blessing at the end of a sermon. Such prayers often have an ineffable, transcendental beauty and meaningfulness. In other contexts, the prayer leader utters an extemporaneous and heartfelt plea for God to help all of us act on the Word and words that we've just heard. Traditions such as this are beautiful and meaningful in a different way—almost as if we are sharing an intimate moment of conversation between the speaker and the Holy One.

There is, however, a third type of closing prayer that seems somewhat disconcerting and to be avoided. It is a variation of the extemporaneous prayer, but it has a different feel than the traditions just mentioned. That feel is difficult to articulate, and I recognize my limitation in describing it. This third type is not so much a closing prayer or heartfelt plea as it is an only slightly abridged replay of the sermon just given. It can be distressing to hear because it doesn't feel at all like a prayer:

> "Dear Heavenly Father, we ask you to help us remember the three main things we heard today. We ask that the "three Ps of Prayer" come to mind when we come before You, ideally each morning in our private time at the start of our day as we have seen in Matthew 6:6-8 and Luke 5:15-16. The first is the Purpose of Prayer; the Second is the Power of Prayer; and the third is the Potential of Prayer. The Purpose of Prayer helps us see the ways in which we should pray according to Your will. We are thankful that you have reminded us of that purpose in Matthew 6:9-13 where Jesus gave us a model of prayer according to Your will, and equally thankful that Deacon Ralph will be leading us into deeper understanding of the Purpose of Prayer on the next three Wednesday evening Bible studies at 7:00pm in the church library. And Father, we know that the Power of Prayer

is unlimited through the many examples you have provided such as in Mark 11:22-25 and James 5:13-18 where we have seen in verse 16 that the prayer of a righteous person is powerful and effective. Finally, the third P of Prayer is the Potential of Prayer . . ."

That above paragraph was particularly difficult to write, likely because it is so painful to hear as the concluding prayer following a sermon. Although it is not a verbatim transcript from any sermon, it is a too-common example of the third type of closing prayer identified in this section. There have been occasions when I wanted to blurt out "Are you *praying*?" as a closing prayer replayed nearly the entire sermon. I think that I—and likely other listeners—have that reaction because what is being spoken seems very unlike a humble plea intended to seek the blessing and guidance of a sovereign God and very much like a calculated rehashing of an entire sermon intended to drive home the speaker's main points. If a sermon should not be a large college economics lecture, a closing prayer should not be the recitation session.

CONCLUSIONS

It is obvious that a sermon is not a lecture. However, there are many aspects of developing and delivering a lecture that can be valuable in their adaptation to developing and delivering a sermon.

Of all chapters in this book, this was the most difficult for me to write. I hope that the principles and ideas presented here are interpreted not as techniques or rules. Rather, they are principles derived from what has been learned about learning and are intended to be applied not as mechanical rules, but as considerations to have in mind when thinking about the content and delivery of a sermon. It is hoped that these points will prompt explicit consideration of important questions such as:

- "Is a deep philological dive a relevant aid to helping listeners grasp and use the bigger point of the sermon or an academic digression?"
- "Am I using the allotted time as efficiently and effectively as possible?"
- "Have I appropriately taken into account how to make the sermon accessible to all listeners, perhaps especially those not intimately connected with church culture and traditions?

Considering these questions and others implied in this chapter can provide a helpful framework for making decisions about what to include, exclude, and how to configure a sermon so that it provides listeners with the greatest opportunity to grasp what is intended, retain that important learning, and be able to apply it in daily life. Although questions such as those just listed are serious and challenging, struggling toward the answers can be of great benefit. We now turn 180 degrees and consider a much less serious, but equally challenging topic: incorporating humor into sermons.

CHAPTER 4

No Laughing Matter

SO A PRIEST, A rabbi, and an imam walk into a bar.

OK . . . I just made that up. I have no idea what a punchline for that joke might be. For purposes of this chapter, however, the punchline is unimportant. The use of humor in sermons might have been included as a topic in the preceding chapter. However, humor is incorporated so ubiquitously—and it is so consequential—that it seemed appropriate to address the topic of humor in its own right.

From the perspective of helping listeners *learn*, humor is a serious thing.

In fact, it is so serious that a spoiler alert is in order, and I'll divulge the punchline of this chapter right off the bat: Humor should *only* be included with a specific purpose. Perhaps surprisingly, that purpose is *not* to make people laugh, it is to help them learn. Used wrongly, humor can actually do more harm than good.

THE CONTEXT OF HUMOR

Who doesn't appreciate a good pun, a humorous anecdote, some levity to break the ice, a light-hearted introduction at the beginning of a homily, or a comedic interjection in the course of an extended and weighty sermon topic? We have all at least heard *attempts* at humor during sermons. Our overall evaluations of those attempts probably vary; based on my own church-going experience, I'd say that most of the time the attempts are successful. For example, I recall being tickled recently by a list of church bulletin typos and awkward usages in church announcements that were recounted to kick off a homily on forgiveness. A sampling of what was presented is shown in Table 4-1.[1] Each entry on the list was well-received, with congregational responses ranging from groans to guffaws; all of them were clean, witty, and entertaining.

Table 4-1

Humorous Typos from Church Bulletins and Announcements

"Please place your donation in the envelope along with the deceased person(s) you want remembered."
"Eight new choir robes are currently needed due to the addition of some new members and to the deterioration of some older ones."
"For those of you who have children and don't know it, we have a nursery downstairs."
"There will be a Bilingual Chicken Dinner this Sunday at Noon."
"The peace-making meeting scheduled for today has been cancelled due to a conflict."
"It's Drug Awareness Week: Get involved in drugs before your children do."
"Let us join David and Lisa in the celebration of their wedding and bring their happiness to a conclusion."
"At the evening service tonight, the sermon topic will be 'What is hell?' Come early and listen to our choir practice."
"Barbara remains in the hospital and needs blood donors for more transfusions. She is also having trouble sleeping and requests tapes of Pastor Nelson's sermons."
"Applications are now being accepted for 2 year old nursery workers."
"The ladies of the church have cast off clothing of every kind. They may be seen in the basement on Friday afternoon."
"The Over 60s Choir will be disbanded for the summer with the thanks of the entire church."

Adapted from "The World's Funniest Church Bulletin Typos."
www.proofreadingservices.com/pages/church-bulletin-typos

1. In trying to track down the source of these quips, I found nearly identical versions on numerous internet sites; no website provided an attribution for the list or claimed authorship. I became skeptical that these "typos" were authentic. Although some of them may have been faithfully reproduced from printed church bulletins or quoted accurately from oral announcements, I suspected that some others were the created by someone with a good sense of humor. Regardless of the source and legitimacy, I had to admit that they *were* funny.

Without question, humor can be a good thing, but like many of the principles of instructional design, it's complicated. It seems somewhat of an oxymoron to write this, but humor has been studied very seriously. Many dry, scholarly studies of humor have been conducted, primarily in the field of psychology. For example, one academic volume has catalogued the different kinds of humor; explored the cognitive origins of humor; probed the social functions of humor; examined the relationships between humor, laughter and smiling; and investigated the ways in which humor is related to our physiological responses to it.[2] In contrast, the use of humor has been addressed quite humorously in other publications and numerous how-to book have been written to help speakers make their presentations more humorous.[3]

THREE PERILS OF HUMOR

Even clean, witty, and entertaining humor must be used cautiously, however, and there are a plethora of potential pitfalls when attempting to incorporate humor into any presentation—perhaps especially so in a sermon. In this section, we'll look at only two of them: one very briefly, and one somewhat more in-depth.

I Don't Get It

The first potential problem that can arise when attempting to include a humorous anecdote, story, joke, pun, or whatever into a sermon is that, well, it won't be funny. I was once on a panel at a large professional meeting where we "roasted" a distinguished senior person in the field on the occasion of his retirement. There were four of us who had been asked to make humorous comments about our colleague in front of an audience of about 1,000 members who were eager to enjoy the retirement roast at the end of a long day of academic presentations.

My hopefully-funny remarks were scheduled as the third presentation, so I was able to get a feel for the other presenters' styles, areas of focus, and audience reactions before I had to speak. The first presenter hit a home

---

2. See Goldstein and McGhee, *The Psychology of Humor;* see also Martin and Ford, *The Psychology of Humor: An Integrative Approach.*

3. See, for example, Berk, *Humor as an Instructional Defibrillator.*

run; her remarks were engaging, edgy, clean, and side-splittingly funny. I was so fully engaged in the frivolity of the moment that, for a moment, I completely forgot the jitters I had about my own upcoming presentation. The second presenter brought back those jitters—in a big way. His remarks weren't biting, sarcastic, mean-spirited, off-color, confusing, or demeaning. They just weren't funny.

It was traumatic to watch a well-respected colleagues' remarks fall so flat. The audience reaction wasn't hostile or rejecting; it just wasn't . . . *anything*. The 12 minutes allocated for his presentation must have seemed like 12 eons to my colleague.[4] Compassion welled up in me (and I suspect in many members of the audience that afternoon) as I vicariously felt the pain of what he must have been experiencing: hoping that the presentation could just end immediately; hoping to escape the punishing silence of the audience; wanting to just slink away; and regretting having agreed to even be on the panel in the first place. Sometimes, trying to be funny is not fun.

In contrast to that professional audience, congregations are probably apt to politely give the benefit of the doubt. In my experience, they are much more likely to chuckle when the drollery door is opened for even the briefest time and to show gratitude for even modest attempts at humor. To their good credit, a lot of church audiences will laugh even when they *don't* think something is funny as a demonstration of kind-heartedness and goodwill toward their pastor, priest, or minister.

A first, innocuous recommendation would be to encourage anyone to experiment with including humor at any appropriate time in a sermon. I think it's nearly impossible for anyone attempting to inject a little humor into a sermon to fall as flat as my colleague did and even the dourest of congregants will likely appreciate the attempt. Like the contemporary genre called Dad Jokes (aka "groaners"), even weak humor can be helpful and embraced in the right circumstances.

Two caveats are necessary to qualify that recommendation. For one, it should be noted that I recommended including humor at *an appropriate time*. I'll have more to say about the timing and content of humor shortly. For another, I also was careful to note that injecting "a *little* humor" can be helpful. No one expects—or wants—a sermon to be an extended comedic performance.

---

4. According to Merriam-Webster dictionary, an eon is "a unit of time equal to a billion years." So, admittedly it's an exaggeration to say that the 12 minutes seemed like 12 billion years, but not much.

Disembodied Humor

Never having attended seminary, I don't know if humor in sermons is encouraged. But *something* is going on. I'm confident that nearly all readers have heard a sermon that began with a funny story, joke, or some other ostensibly harmless icebreaker. However, what on the surface seems *innocuous*, might actually be nocuous. This happens routinely when the point of the humor is not connected to the main learning that the sermon is attempting to foster.

I recall a particularly powerful example of this phenomenon. The speaker had a great icebreaker in the following anecdote:

> An elderly couple were sitting in their living room one evening. The husband was sipping on some wine; the wife was doing some reading. At some point late into the evening, the husband said softly, "I really love you." Hearing the romantic utterance, his wife asked: "Oh, Harold, is that you talking, or just the wine?" His reply: "Oh, I'm sorry, Martha. That was me talking *to* the wine." Many listeners chuckled, and the speaker proceeded to the meat of the sermon.

The problem? There are several, actually. First, an anecdote that was intended to be humorous was only mildly so; the fact that only a portion of the congregation responded may have meant that some likely found the joke to be sexist. It may have touched a nerve in families dealing with substance abuse. For our purposes, however, a major issue is that the humor was not connected to the main idea of the sermon. Honestly, I don't recall the main point of the sermon—and *that's the problem*. If there is one consensus principle about the use of humor to promote learning, it is this: it is essential for any humor to be explicitly connected to the intended learning, such that when the joke or humorous story is recalled by a listener, the intended point will be remembered also. Icebreakers that seem harmless might unwittingly be working against the main ideas that a homilist is trying to communicate.

Humor that Hurts

A third peril to be avoided when incorporating humor in a sermon is that the attempt at humor might not simply be un-funny, but there is the omnipresent potential for attempted humor to be offensive. One such attempt at humor in a sermon recently garnered national attention in network news outlets for its offensiveness.[5] This particularly painful example was drawn from the sermon of a Malden, Missouri pastor; it was widely reported across the U.S. and memorialized in a viral video. In his sermon, the pastor was ostensibly trying to help strengthen marriages in the local church by, among other things, encouraging women to look attractive for their husbands.

Even as I typed that last sentence, it just felt uncomfortable and like trouble was just around the corner. What came to mind were so many ways that topic could go wrong. Nonetheless, the pastor pressed on. Among several ill-fated attempts at humor to support points in the sermon, he dropped the following "joke": What's the difference between a man's fiancée and his wife? About 60 pounds.[6]

The unanimity and vociferousness of criticisms were well-deserved. I don't think the person *meant* harm, but it's difficult to understand how such an attempt at humor would not be received as hurtful, disparaging, demeaning, and sexist. When I last checked, the pastor was officially on leave and seeking professional counseling.

To be sure, few attempts at humor are this egregiously wrong. Nonetheless, it is still essential to scrupulously examine *all* attempted humor for its potential to be hurtful to persons and harmful to the intended point of a sermon. Returning to that humorous list of typos and usage errors shown in Table 4-1 provides a context for examining such potential. It's not possible to make generic judgments about humor; however, it is essential to take into account a sermon's audience as described in Chapter 2. In looking at that list of typos, it seems important—before including such humor in a sermon—to reflect on the potential to offend, alienate, or demean.

Let's consider two examples. For one, some entries in Table 4-1 appear to portray older church members portrayed as doddering. For another, some entries seem disparaging of members who serve in the choir. The context of a pastor's relationship with the elderly, the choir (or whatever persons are the referent in a joke), as well as the relationship with the broader congregation and the spirit in which such quips were delivered can make the difference between a light-hearted moment for everyone and an

---

5. An easy rule of thumb is to avoid including anything in a sermon if, as in this example, one would not want it to be circulated in network new outlets or go viral in social media!

6. Adapted from Fieldstadt, "Missouri Pastor on Leave."

interjection that may be hurtful to some and unintentionally distract from the learning goals of a sermon.

Humor *can* be used beneficially to promote learning, retention, and application of important spiritual perspectives. However, a major concern with incorporating humor in a sermon is that there is such expansive potential for it to be offensive. The list of landmines is nearly endless: humor that relies on distinctions based on gender, age, ethnicity, disability, language, cognitive ability, physical appearance, occupation, and myriad other characteristics is almost certainly going to be offensive to some listeners.

Of the two concerns about humor addressed here, this second potentiality is the much more serious concern. It is difficult to always know whether something might be misunderstood, taken wrongly, not as intended, or as an offense by a listener. One such attempt at humor can unintentionally but completely derail any chance of a listener gaining from a sermon what was intended; a 37-second anecdote intended as humor can negate the entirety of a 37-minute sermon that was otherwise spot on.

A version of the Hippocratic Oath from the field of medicine is relevant as a recommendation for homiletical humor: "First do no harm." To help inform the evaluation of whether a humorous reference should be included in a sermon, one of the easiest strategies is to ask one or more congregants to provide an *a priori*, candid critique. Ideally, the polled parties would not only be members of the church with some knowledge of its history, but also be able to reflect the perspectives of any group that may be sensitive to the attempted humor. Of course, power relationships may be at play in such a request. The most secure and well-meaning member of a church might still be reluctant to offer an unvarnished reaction to the spiritual leadership of that church regarding some humor proposed for a sermon. If the potential effect of including some contemplated humor is in question, the same simple guideline cited in Chapter 3 is also appropriate here: "When in doubt, leave it out."

HUMOR THAT HELPS

At the beginning of this chapter, it was noted that the primary purpose of including humor in a sermon is *not* to make people laugh. That assertion might strike some readers as curious or wrong on its face. However, there is a strong case to be made for that assertion. Here is another principle from instructional design: to best promote learning, humor should be considered for inclusion only to the extent that it supports the intended main point of the sermon. That is a difficult but not impossible criterion to satisfy. Before providing some examples of how to accomplish it, I'll take a moment to first detail how humor that fails to meet that criterion can go awry. I'll begin by relating my recollection of one of the most humorous anecdotes I've ever heard as part of a sermon.[7]

The setting for the humor was described as a Sunday school class for a group of about a dozen 6-year-olds. The Sunday school teacher, Mrs. Manton, was attempting to begin the class with something that the children would find to be a fun and easy Q&A warm-up activity. The teacher told the children that she would be describing something and that the first child to answer each question correctly would get a special prize. For the first question, the teacher said,

"What I'm thinking of is furry. It is small. It can be brown or black. It can climb trees. It has a bushy tail. It buries acorn nuts in the fall and digs them up in the spring . . ."

Some of the children appeared reluctant to make a guess, so the teacher looked around the room. The teacher noticed that one little girl, Elaina, had a particularly troubled look on her face. However, the teacher knew Elaina to be typically engaged and she believed that Elaina would be likely to answer the first question correctly, thereby encouraging the other children to join in for the questions that would follow. Despite Elaina's apparently troubled countenance, the teacher asked:

"Elaina, what do you think?"

The little girl paused before answering; her voice was not confident and tinged with some anxiety:

"Oh, Mrs. Manton, I'm confused. I know the right answer is 'Jesus,' but it sure sounds like a squirrel to me."

For readers with experience teaching Sunday school, that context and anecdote are probably familiar, humorous, and perhaps somewhat discouraging at the same time. That humorous story about Elaina has helped me in my own teaching with its clear message that, sometimes, we can create a context where we unintentionally communicate that the "right" answer is always well-known, always the same, traditional, or universal. Without meaning to do so, we can thwart clarity of thought, critical thinking, or divergent perspectives on a question. Elaina *knew* that the right answer to just about every question in her Sunday school was "Jesus." She was reluctant to give any other response that didn't conform to that norm.

---

7. I don't recall it being clarified at the time, but my sense is that the anecdote is a humorous story only, not a true historical event.

Here's the real punchline to that anecdote. As best I can remember, on the Sunday I heard the squirrel story, the pastor indicated that his sermon was going to focus on forgiveness. One of my own children and I had both been struggling with issues around forgiveness, so I was interested, invested, and incented to learn what the pastor wanted us to learn about that topic. Unfortunately, I have no recollection of what I was supposed to learn about forgiveness; the only lasting takeaway I have from that Sunday is a really funny squirrel joke.

In fairness, I can't ascribe all culpability for my lack of learning to the homilist that day. Listeners have responsibilities for attending, organizing, and sifting what they hear. Additionally, in any specific context, not all listeners will be affected in the same way. I suspect that many congregants that Sunday learned something important about forgiveness. All of those factors notwithstanding, there is an important instructional design principle at play in this situation that speaks to the inclusion of humor: *the primary purpose of including humor is to aid in the learning, recall, or application of the main point of the sermon.*

That is what I meant earlier when I wrote that the main purpose of including humor in a sermon was not to make people laugh. Humor should be used strategically to support a bigger idea. Hearing humor should reinforce the main point during a sermon, Remembering a joke or humorous story should bring to mind the main point afterward. Failure to consider and structure a sermon along these lines risks that the humor will actually interfere with the intended learning and, like what happened to me, result in recall of the joke, not the point.

What does this look like? Here are two examples, one from the distant past of my experience, one more recent.

The first is related to a point made in the previous chapter about Christian jargon. Just as with jargon, it seems easy sometimes to reply with a trite response, whether by habit or without a lot of thought. The intended point of a sermon I heard was that we should avoid such responses because they can be interpreted as empty at best, and perhaps dangerous at worst—as the following humorous anecdote suggests. At the beginning of the sermon, the pastor recounted the story of a preacher who, in his first weeks in a new pastorate at a small, country church, was given the gift of a riding horse by a generous member:

> *Before leaving the horse with the preacher, the congregant instructed the preacher in the unusual way the horse had been trained for riding. Instead of the traditional commands of "giddy up" to get the*

> *horse to run, and "whoa" to get the horse to stop, the horse had been trained to respond to "Praise the Lord!" and "Amen!" respectively.*
>
> *Later that week, the new preacher had some free time to take the horse for a first ride on a nearby trail. He climbed into the saddle and said, "Giddy up." Of course, the horse didn't move. He then gave a somewhat louder "Giddy up!" accompanied by a nudge of his heel to the horse's ribs. Still no movement.*
>
> *Finally, the preacher remembered: "Praise the Lord," the preacher said, and the horse obligingly took off like a shot. The horse maintained a smooth, full-on racing gallop along the trail.*
>
> *Approaching quickly in the near distance, the preacher noticed that the trail dropped off. As the horse and rider got quickly closer, the preacher could see the impending danger of a 300-foot cliff. "Whoa," he said to the horse with no response. "Whoa!" he said again. The horse kept racing toward the cliff. "Whoa! Whoa!" the preacher yelled.*
>
> *At the last minute—and now fearing for his life—the terrified preacher remembered the instruction he'd been given and desperately yelled "AMEN!" The horse came to an abrupt halt just a foot from the edge of the cliff.*
>
> *"Oh, Praise the Lord!" the preacher exclaimed.*

Perhaps it goes without saying, but the humorous anecdote about the country preacher and the horse was intended by the homilist to help listeners lock in his main point: our words should be chosen carefully; we should avoid using expressions cavalierly; our words can have consequences. For a sermon, however, it is an important principle that this does *not* go without saying! Here is the relevant learning principle: The reason behind including the humor should be made, explained, and explicitly linked to the main idea.

It is crucial to note that the preceding anecdote was executed to perfectly align to that principle. It was selected judiciously and inserted strategically within the sermon. Building on the idea of an advance organizer described earlier in this book, the pastor first introduced listeners to the main point about being cautious in what we say. The point was made at the beginning of the sermon to help listeners organize what was to come. I don't recall this detail precisely, but the key text for the sermon may well have been Ephesians 4:29: "Do not let any unwholesome talk come out of your mouths, but only what is helpful for building others up according to their needs, that it may benefit those who listen." (In retrospect, it would seem particularly appropriate, humorous, and related to the demise of the country preacher if the key text had Proverbs 18:21a: "The tongue can bring death or life.")

Here's the more crucial note: After retelling the anecdote about the country preacher and the horse, the pastor then connected the dots for listeners. In this example, the *reason* for including the humor was made explicit: the country preacher was careless, cavalier, or not thoughtful about the use of the phrase, "Praise the Lord." Although similar casual usage is not likely to cost us our lives like the preacher who presumably met his demise going over a cliff, the pastor was trying to help us learn that we should not be flippant about praise for our Creator, we should not speak without thinking about our words, or without considering the consequences of our speech on those who hear it—horses or persons!

In short, the prescription for humorous medicine is threefold: 1) a framework for the humor should be provided; 2) the humor should reinforce the main point, with the goal of making the main point more memorable or useful; and 3) the connections between the humor and the main point should be made explicitly.[8]

These three elements relate to the topic of advance organizers described in Chapter 2. The first element helps listeners hang the new sport shirt—that is, the main point about monitoring our words—in an area where it can easily be found and used. The second element helps link the memory of the anecdote to the intended main point. In the days and weeks after a sermon is delivered, listeners who recall the joke will recall the main point and vice versa.

Regarding the third element in that prescription—making the connections explicit—there is not only support found in principles of instructional design, but Jesus himself practiced this on many occasions. Perhaps one of the most familiar examples of this is found in the parable of the sower (Matthew 13:4-8). In the parable, Jesus relates a parable involving a farmer who sowed seeds that fell on different types of ground. Some of the seed fell on a path where it was eaten by birds; some fell on rocky ground where it initially sprang up but quickly died because it could not establish deep roots in the rocky soil and was scorched by the sun; other seed fell

---

8. In several places in this book, I have referenced the excellent work of Haddon Robinson whose book, *Biblical Preaching*, has been rightfully regarded as foundational reading for generations of preachers-in-training. Robinson argues the opposite of what I have presented here, noting: "If the illustration needs to be explained to make it clear, it should not be used," 151. Whereas generally eschewing illustrations that are left underdeveloped or unclear seems wise, careful explication and clarification of a memorable narrative such as that of the sower is often not only helpful but necessary.

among weeds which choked out the new growth; still other seed fell on good soil where it produced an abundant crop.

Jesus recognized that many agrarian listeners would readily be able to comprehend the story. However, he didn't want them to just remember the story for its own sake. The story was only spoken as an aid to learning the important point he was trying to make. Thus, he took time to explain the parable to his audience and to make connections between the anecdote and the overarching point. Notice in the Scriptural portion that follows the parable the care Jesus took to explicitly link each part of the parable to the point he was trying to help his listeners grasp. Jesus said:

> "Listen then to what the parable of the sower means: When anyone hears the message about the kingdom and does not understand it, the evil one comes and snatches away what was sown in their heart. *This is the seed sown along the path. The seed falling on rocky ground refers to someone who hears the word and at once receives it with joy. But since they have no root, they last only a short time.* When trouble or persecution comes because of the word, they quickly fall away. *The seed falling among the thorns refers to someone who hears the word, but the worries of this life and the deceitfulness of wealth choke the word,* making it unfruitful. But *the seed falling on good soil refers to someone who hears the word and understands it.* This is the one who produces a crop, yielding a hundred, sixty or thirty times what was sown."[9]

A final point is that humor does not only refer to spoken words. All of the same principles described here apply equally to visual presentation of humor. With the increasing use of PowerPoint® slides, YouTube® videos, and other graphics, it is likely that humor presented in a visual mode will be incorporated even more frequently. I'll describe two examples of visual humor, one less effective, one more effective.[10]

One medium for visual humor employs the oft-seen portable marquee boards that are used for advertising at various businesses, to promote

---

9. Matthew 13:18–23 (NIV), emphasis added.

10. By this time, many readers will have noted two additional principles of learning that I have employed a number of times in this book, but I will emphasize them here. The first principle is that giving examples is extremely helpful in aiding listeners to learn. Diverse, realistic, practical examples drawn from the lived experiences of those involved (i.e., the speaker or the members of the congregation) best support the intended learning. Second, to cement a difficult concept, it is often beneficial to give one or more examples of what something *is*, or how it applies, followed by examples of what it is *not*, or situations in which it should not be applied. This so-called *example/non-example* principle is exceptionally powerful.

political candidates, or for highlighting announcements about upcoming events. Examples of this kind of visual humor seem to be fairly common. I imagine nearly all of us have seen humorous sayings posted close to the street in or near a church parking lot. The marquees contain clever phrasings such as *"Seven Days without Prayer Makes One Weak"* or *"C H _ R C H. The only thing missing is U."* One of my favorites is a sign I recall seeing about 20 years ago that proclaimed: "Your Choice for Eternity: Smoking or Non-Smoking." Each of these has in common that they are somewhat humorous as intended and likely memorable.

One of the most delightful examples I have seen of visual humor is shown in Figure 4-1. It also involves a mobile marquee; the image was sent to me by my brother who lives in southern Michigan where he spotted the sign announcing the monthly fish fry at a local Knights of Columbus hall. This image is a particularly good example of the effective use of humor. The sign also incorporates the principles covered in this chapter. It is not offensive; it is actually humorous; and it has the intended effect on viewers' learning. That is, when hearing the familiar song, "Our God is an Awesome God," the church fish fry will almost certainly come to mind.

Figure 4-1

Example of Visual Humor

CONCLUSIONS

Humor can be an effective tool for helping listeners learn an essential point in a sermon. Ironically, for humor to be effective, it is only somewhat necessary that it is actually funny. It is certainly more enjoyable for listeners if it *is* funny, but it is not the most important consideration. More important is that the humorous foray is not offensive and that it does not interfere with or detract from the intended focus of a sermon. In most situations, if there is doubt about whether the joke, anecdote, or quip is benign, it is wise to get a second opinion. Humor included in a sermon should be chosen because it can be tightly linked to the point that the speaker intends for listeners to learn, remember, and use. Always explicitly connect the dots for listeners. When including something humorous in a sermon, and in order to help listeners lock in the main point, the relationship between the humor and the point should be made abundantly clear.

CHAPTER 5

Vehicles

I SHOULD BE EMBARRASSED to write this chapter.

The purpose of the following sections is to provide some guidelines related to best practices involving the mechanisms, platforms, applications, and conveyances used for communicating in sermons. However, if any of the graduate students in my courses at the University of North Carolina learned that I'd written such a chapter, they might smirk. Several years ago, a good-natured but candid critique appeared in my end-of-semester teaching evaluations when a doctoral student commented that "Dr. Cizek's idea of a multimedia presentation is two colors of chalk."

That still brings a mild sting . . . but also a chuckle. I think what she meant by her comment was that, if my academic knowledge and skills were ranked, expertise in modern instructional technologies would not be near the top of the list.

I also think she underestimated me.

By both choice and circumstance, I've graduated from exclusive use yellow and white chalk for my presentations, and I have tried to master many of the current technologies for effective teaching and learning in the 21st century. In my own work, in addition to hundreds of presentations for lectures, I have created and delivered over 200 presentations at research conferences associated with my professional academic life. I have focused on recognizing the difference between what is germane and what is gimmicky in a presentation, what is helpful and what is a hindrance. And, although my pedagogical skills were acquired in the face-to-face chalkboard teaching era, I have benefited from what instructional designers have learned about technology and teaching in (especially) the post-Covid times. In this chapter, we'll look at some principles for effective teaching and preaching that incorporate some of that knowledge.

THE CONTEMPORARY CONTEXT

Just like instructors at a modern university, pastors have many options for instructional technology tools available to them, ranging from the mundane to the mesmerizing: Tik Tok videos, zoom, iclickers, Jamboards, Instagram, prezi, virtual reality, even (God forbid) AI generated sermon content. It seems impossible that anyone could master all of the available communication technologies. Thankfully, they are not all necessary. A somewhat narrower set of tools—tools that are appropriate and perhaps essential to communicate well—is typically applied in both sermons and professional presentations. Thankfully, researchers have also studied how best to incorporate and use these tools.

Thinking about the changes in instructional technologies that I've witnessed over my teaching career, three things have become clear to me. First, the variety of presentation modes has never been more diverse. Second, diverse presentation formats are increasingly incorporated in sermons, Sunday school classrooms, and Christian education generally. I suspect there are several reasons for this transformation; at least partly, I think, it has been due to tacit listener expectations, subtle pressures for sermons to appear relevant/contemporary, and evolving norms that dictate such diverse and attention-grabbing media be included.[1] Third, there is no reason *not* to embrace existing and emerging instructional technology options to the extent that they provide powerful tools for presenting the Gospel.

It is beyond the scope of this book to consider the social, ethical, or other aspects of a world that hurtles toward seemingly uncritical embrace of facial recognition, digital currency, genetic manipulation, artificial intelligence and—it seems—whatever a technology can be developed to do in any sphere of human life. Those relentless impulses aside, the third point in the preceding paragraph is the most relevant for considering how to develop and deliver better sermons and it is a critical criterion to apply to any

---

1. One commonly hears the eulogy for traditional sermons along the lines of "The era of talking heads is dead." However, I think the rumors of the demise are greatly exaggerated. I—and probably all serious listeners—will always prefer a "talking head" that delivers a clear, compelling, actionable message over a technology-enhanced spectacle of little substance or spiritual impact.

use of multimedia or other technologies. There is a litmus test related to the learning emphasis of this book: Does the use of the technology serve to advance listener comprehension, retention, and action with respect to the intended Gospel message?

All of that said, I suspect that many readers of this chapter and I will have at least four things in common:

1) we know that modern instructional technologies are powerful and can be masterfully enlisted to support the learning that a sermon intends to produce;

2) we have seen those technologies work both well and badly;

3) we struggle in the same ways to keep pace with emerging instructional technologies; and

4) we recognize that the medium cannot become, but must only serve and support, the message.

As another aspect of context, let us consider the diversity of modern preaching venues and the technologies that must be leveraged in those places to promote effective communication. According to Thomas Long, "Preachers still hold forth in old country churches and neo-Gothic sanctuaries, but they are almost as likely to be found in taverns and movie theaters, storefronts and living rooms."[2] I've never worshipped in a tavern, but my wife and I have attended church services in locations ranging from awe-inspiring cathedrals to what appeared to have formerly been an ethnic grocery store in an urban strip mall.

As an additional contextual dimension, it is relevant to consider the myriad ways in which the pandemic of 2020 has altered the way in which sermons have been delivered via technologies such as podcasts and Facebook livestreams. Even in pre-pandemic times, sermons increasingly expanded the menu of media incorporated in their presentation to include presentation software, video, live streamed segments, and other technologies. Covid simply accelerated the pace. The rapid ecclesiastical incorporation of these technologies in response to the pandemic has—for better and worse—affected how church communities interact, how liturgies are structured, and how sermons are delivered. It seems almost certain that those technologies and effects will linger well after the pandemic has passed.

---

2. Long, *The Witness of Preaching*, xi.

Vehicles

Finally, a note on what falls under the umbrella term of "technology." The Merriam-Webster dictionary describes *technology* in a way that is much broader than the usual connotations that come to mind; it defines technology broadly as "the practical application of knowledge especially in a particular area." Thus, whereas multimedia presentations come readily to mind as an instructional technology, there are many other vehicles that can contribute powerfully to the opportunities for listeners to learn, retain, and use what is presented in a sermon. For example, the field of instructional design provides guidance on the technologies of stories, analogies, examples, and other such tools. Many sermons routinely incorporate these. Attention to how best to incorporate technology tools can also maximize the effectiveness of sermons.

The balance of this chapter focuses on two main avenues that are likely to be most frequently used, most misused, and yet most promising in terms of their potential to aid learners. First up are the ubiquitous PowerPoint® presentations.[3] We will then consider images and stories as avenues to promote retention and action on sermon content. One note: the content of the following section is not limited specifically to the branded PowerPoint software, but it applies to any of the several alternatives to that application. Many engaging alternatives to standard PowerPoint templates and presentation styles exist. Table 5-1 provides a listing of a few alternatives along with brief annotations on each.

---

3. Henceforth, the more general terms *slides* or *slide deck* will be used instead of the more cumbersome to read, write, and typeset proprietary terms and associated registered trademark indicators.

Table 5-1
Some Alternatives to PowerPoint Templates

Alternative	Source	Notes
Google Slides	www.google.com	Essentially the Google version of PowerPoint, Google Slides is a web-based presentation program available as one of the dozens of free apps accessible from the Google home page. Registration of a Google account is required.
Canva	www.canva.com	Canva is broader than merely a presentation program, referring to itself as a comprehensive design tool. According to the website, it is "free for life."
Keynote	www.apple.com/keynote/	Designed primarily for Apple products, Keynote is another basic slide deck utility, similar to PowerPoint. A basic version is free.
Slides Carnival	www.slidescarnival.com/	A source for free PowerPoint and Google Slides templates/themes.
Prezi Present	https://prezi.com	About as different from PowerPoint as you can get. Rather than offering a linear slide-by-slide presentation, it's more of a non-linear, visual and interactive map, wherein viewers interact with different elements on a virtual canvas. A free trial is available; a basic version for personal use costs $5/month.
Mentimeter	www.mentimeter.com/	Mentimeter provides a basic alternative to PowerPoint for slide presentations. Though possible of interest only in certain contexts, the free version also enables uses to create "Questions" and "Quizzes" for obtaining feedback from an audience.
Vyond	www.vyond.com	For those interested in a presentation platform that is video based (as opposed to basic slides) Vyond provides a fairly easy to use utility for creating video presentations. A free trial is available; the basic version carries an annual fee of $299.

SLIDE DECK PRESENTATIONS

There are many advantages to incorporating a projected slide presentation into a sermon and such adjuncts are increasingly used across denominations. Research in the learning sciences has demonstrated that using multiple receptive modalities (e.g., simultaneously engaging the dual learning modalities of listening and viewing) when presenting a sermon promote better comprehension and recall than the use of a single modality (e.g., listening alone). The very act of preparing and rehearsing a slide deck presentation forces a speaker to evaluate and adjust the organization, pace, timing, and content of the presentation.

During a presentation, the slides can function in much the same way as a set of notes, aiding the presenter in sequencing the next point to be made, prompting recall of the next example, and ensuring the accuracy of a quotation. For those attending a sermon, slides can incorporate a variety of elements, including tables, audio, graphics, pictures, motion, and other devices that can help to maintain interest, focus, and attention. Slides can help ensure that all in attendance are at least presented with common message elements. Done properly, slides can make the experience of a sermon more accessible for those with hearing loss or visual disability. Projected content can aid those whose late arrival resulted in seating in an area with poor acoustics.

A slide deck presentation has many potential pitfalls as well. The mere availability of a presentation technology does not mean it should be used or foregrounded. As Robinson has observed decades ago, "Undoubtedly, modern techniques can enhance communication, but on the other hand, they can substitute for the message—the startling and unusual may mask a vacuum."[4] Beyond mistaking the medium for the message, there are manifold ways-to-go-wrong creating and presenting a slide deck; the number of books and other resources that have been produced to help presenters avoid them is evidence of that. Because that terrain has been so well-charted by others, I'll avoid addressing many of those pitfalls in this chapter. Similarly, a wealth of expert advice exists for creating effective, accessible, impactful slide presentations. Interested readers may want to consult a comprehensive resource describing these practical strategies such as:

---

4. Robinson, *Biblical Preaching*, 16.

- *Presentation Zen*[5]
- *The Compelling Communicator: Mastering the Art and Science of Exceptional Presentation Design*[6]
- *Teaching in a Digital Age: Guidelines for Designing Teaching and Learning*[7] and
- *Tips for Making Effective PowerPoint Presentations.*[8]

The balance of this chapter will address four aspects of slide deck creation and use that are most applicable to sermons and to aiding listeners/viewers to learn from them. The following sections consider four guidelines that can be easily implemented to promote accessible, engaging, and application-oriented learning from slide presentations.

Density

A slide that is overly dense with words, pictures, graphics, animations—any text and visual material—fails on so many counts. From simply a visual perspective, crowding material onto a slide requires the use of small images, small fonts, small borders, crowding—all of which can make a slide impossible to see/read, distracting, too cognitively taxing for viewers to process accurately and, ultimately, ignorable. To the extent that a slide is included because it contains some key information the speaker wants the listeners to learn, that objective may not be realized.

I imagine that many readers have had the same frustrating experience that I have had on far too many occasions when attending a professional presentation. Three situations underlie that frustration: one reflects a sin of omission; the other two illustrate sins of commission.

In the first situation, a presenter simply isn't aware that the presentation is overly dense. In such cases, those in the audience can simply be adrift because they are unable to see the presented material, especially if the spoken content does not repeat what is on the slides. At one conference,

---

5. Reynolds, *Presentation Zen.*
6. Pollard, *The Compelling Communicator.*
7. Bates, *Teaching in a Digital Age.*
8. National Conference of State Legislatures, *Tips for Making Effective PowerPoint Presentations.*

a person who I'll refer to as "Speaker 1" wanted to share specific examples of elementary school students' reactions to a new mathematics curriculum. The students apparently liked the new way of teaching but, as can be seen—or *not seen!*—in Figure 5-1, it was impossible to discern that from the slide that was used. Apparently, Speaker 1 had not done a trial run of the slides in the venue where the presentation would be given—the sin of omission—and was unaware that the audience could not read any of the content on the slides. Because Speaker 1 did not read the slides to the audience, they were unable to learn anything from the projected student comments.

Figure 5-1

> The primary results of this research are well captured by the several comments of our research participants. We conducted extensive, triangulated interviews that resulted in rich data that pointed to several grounded conclusions. We will quote the comments of several of our participants that led us to various and educationally-actionable conclusions. For example, one of our participants was a student from a low-SES rural 2nd grade classroom who described in detail his feelings about the mathematics interventions that were introduced early in the year in the classroom of Cooperating Teacher A . (We have substituted letters for names to ensure all participants confidentiality and anonymity pursuant to our IRB approval conditions and to protect and respect the rights of all participants. We think that this student's comments provide new insights into the effectiveness and potential of our ineffectiveness of current practices, but the potential for increased learning if new paradigms are adopted. Our first participant spoke passionately about this conjoining of content and affective aims. Accordingly, in the words of Participant 1:
>
> **Participant 1:** "I really like math now. The new things our teacher is doing are really helping me to know more math and do better on my tests and homework assignments."
>
> Another one of our participants provided unique insights into the secondary results of this research which are also well captured by the several comments of our research participants. We conducted extensive, triangulated interviews that resulted in rich data that pointed to several grounded conclusions. We will quote the comments of several of our participants that led us to various and educationally-actionable conclusions. For example, one of our participants was a student from a low-SES rural 2nd grade commercial textbook publishers have uniformly failed to realize not only the ineffectiveness of current practices, but the potential for increased learning if new paradigms are adopted. Our first participant spoke passionately about this conjoining of content and affective aims. Accordingly, in the words of Participant 2:
>
> **Participant 2:** "I feel like I am really getting better at math because of all the math we are doing in class. My teacher is teaching math and I feel like I am learning math. Sometimes we do more math than we used to do. I am learning that math is really important if you want to go to college. Even if you don't want to go to college, math is good because it makes you do stuff like addition, subtraction, multiplying, dividing, and fractions and other stuff, which might come in handy when I'm older in case I need to do stuff like adding, subtracting, multiplication, grouping a bunch of colored blocks into smaller groups of blocks, or when you need to cut a pizza into slices that's fair to you and all your friends like when you are having a birthday party with six friends and you have one pizza, but you're gonna need seven pieces, or maybe even more pieces if your friends are really hungry, so it's a good skill to know that 1/7 is not really as big a piece of pizza as 1/9, or maybe your just gonna need to buy two pizzas if you have to cut it into ninths, or maybe it's like you should say to your parents: "can't you just get me an my friends each our own pizza so we don't have to worry about cutting this pizza into sevenths? So overall, math is really good for you and your parents, I guess."

A LOT of Words on a Slide

At another conference, the presenter, "Speaker 2," wanted to show the data used for a sophisticated quantitative technique called semantic network statistical analysis.[9] That slide, shown in Figure 5-2, was overwhelmed not with words but with numbers. The result of Speaker 2's presentation

---

9. Semantic network analysis is a statistical tool for examining the logical and linguistic relationships between concepts, for example, in a text. The data sets for semantic network analysis are huge, and the analyses are highly computationally intensive. Yes, I know what you are thinking and, regardless of research background, *everyone* has the same question: "Why in the world would anyone want to show the data used for a semantic network analysis?" Answer: I have no idea.

was the same as was the case for Speaker 1—inaccessibility to the audience—but with one difference. In this case, Speaker 2 must have realized in advance that it would be difficult for the audience to make sense of a slide packed with tiny numbers, so a slide that showed the visual results of the network analysis (see Figure 5-3) was shown for clarification. That slide showed the typical output of such an analysis, which consists of an extremely dense collection of lines connecting words and concepts used in a text, with the size, direction, and angles of the lines having specialized meaning. I use the term "clarification" with some sarcasm: the projected image of the network was as equally packed with graphical material as was the slide with students' comments—and equally impossible for viewers to interpret. The situation involving Speaker 2 might be labeled the venial variety of the sins of commission: the presenter had some realization of the presentation deficiency and at least made some attempt to atone for it.

Figure 5-2

0.00235	0.00032	0.00008	0.00006	0.00005	0.00012	0.00005	0.00006	0.00013	0.00012	0.00019	0.00033
0.00679	0.00171	0.00056	0.00039	0.00031	0.00032	0.00039	0.00051	0.00075	0.00060	0.00083	0.00132
0.02056	0.00683	0.00253	0.00165	0.00186	0.00152	0.00182	0.00204	0.00249	0.00195	0.00222	0.00384
0.04630	0.01770	0.00725	0.00517	0.00438	0.00531	0.00539	0.00503	0.00536	0.00467	0.00481	0.00732
0.08551	0.04097	0.01833	0.01350	0.01346	0.01360	0.01287	0.01125	0.01418	0.01071	0.01047	0.01411
0.14064	0.07900	0.04034	0.02987	0.03253	0.02966	0.02301	0.02176	0.02157	0.01873	0.01833	0.02161
0.17842	0.12578	0.07372	0.06219	0.05959	0.05465	0.05614	0.03879	0.03541	0.02891	0.02791	0.03025
0.21520	0.16773	0.11413	0.10810	0.10277	0.09815	0.09527	0.06396	0.05518	0.04223	0.03730	0.03732
0.22748	0.20849	0.15365	0.14808	0.15013	0.13836	0.14320	0.10722	0.08433	0.05451	0.05090	0.04696
0.25485	0.23176	0.18181	0.18328	0.19727	0.19712	0.19022	0.15374	0.12036	0.09134	0.06764	0.06032
0.24929	0.24064	0.19235	0.19839	0.21755	0.23885	0.21632	0.18571	0.15845	0.10862	0.08737	0.07569
0.25728	0.24807	0.19752	0.20233	0.22938	0.23242	0.21289	0.20519	0.16494	0.13451	0.10784	0.09044
0.25448	0.23950	0.18512	0.19253	0.22118	0.21945	0.19960	0.19691	0.19196	0.15120	0.12514	0.10263
0.24684	0.23228	0.17418	0.16955	0.19153	0.19718	0.15983	0.17643	0.18772	0.15697	0.12179	0.11178
0.23496	0.22676	0.15670	0.14585	0.16494	0.16376	0.14447	0.14980	0.16662	0.15183	0.14545	0.11618
0.23023	0.19468	0.13960	0.11992	0.13505	0.13156	0.11902	0.12056	0.13826	0.13572	0.12402	0.11320
0.22697	0.19375	0.12808	0.09665	0.10616	0.10529	0.08651	0.08775	0.10366	0.11277	0.11077	0.10664
0.21584	0.17867	0.11099	0.07521	0.08294	0.08339	0.06620	0.06609	0.08345	0.09157	0.09377	0.09598
0.20733	0.18191	0.09713	0.05983	0.06207	0.06334	0.04957	0.04433	0.06253	0.07255	0.07783	0.07446
0.20255	0.14876	0.08522	0.04631	0.04620	0.04787	0.03558	0.03416	0.04580	0.05369	0.06094	0.07175
0.18724	0.13406	0.06566	0.03575	0.03370	0.03485	0.02564	0.02451	0.03200	0.03924	0.04601	0.05267
0.17615	0.11701	0.06030	0.02896	0.02456	0.02509	0.01935	0.01636	0.02183	0.02833	0.03418	0.04100
0.16762	0.10473	0.04934	0.02221	0.01717	0.01808	0.01377	0.01160	0.01490	0.01911	0.02370	0.02913
0.14568	0.08974	0.03974	0.01740	0.01203	0.01250	0.00974	0.00800	0.00913	0.01274	0.01638	0.02044
0.13340	0.07704	0.03093	0.01352	0.00839	0.00840	0.00688	0.00548	0.00674	0.00845	0.01070	0.01394
0.11567	0.08228	0.02408	0.00909	0.00577	0.00553	0.00444	0.00346	0.00424	0.00528	0.00688	0.00892
0.09012	0.04642	0.01660	0.00711	0.00405	0.00356	0.00278	0.00227	0.00247	0.00303	0.00405	0.00528
0.06854	0.03302	0.01145	0.00475	0.00259	0.00225	0.00186	0.00146	0.00158	0.00174	0.00228	0.00293
0.04669	0.01975	0.00673	0.00285	0.00150	0.00122	0.00101	0.00077	0.00076	0.00086	0.00124	0.00153
0.02993	0.01204	0.00368	0.00158	0.00090	0.00071	0.00048	0.00039	0.00039	0.00040	0.00056	0.00076
0.01714	0.00539	0.00174	0.00084	0.00039	0.00043	0.00024	0.00020	0.00017	0.00016	0.00023	0.00031
0.00948	0.00271	0.00086	0.00038	0.00020	0.00018	0.00010	0.00007	0.00007	0.00007	0.00009	0.00011
0.00591	0.00119	0.00037	0.00027	0.00011	0.00009	0.00004	0.00004	0.00004	0.00002	0.00003	0.00004
0.00426	0.00075	0.00023	0.00010	0.00006	0.00005	0.00002	0.00001	0.00001	0.00001	0.00001	0.00002
0.01483	0.00134	0.00043	0.00024	0.00008	0.00007	0.00002	0.00001	0.00001	0.00001	0.00001	0.00002
4.71653	3.85059	2.36953	2.00390	2.13926	2.13434	1.90341	1.74652	1.76397	1.54265	1.42170	1.35918

A Lot of Numbers on a Slide

Vehicles

Figure 5-3

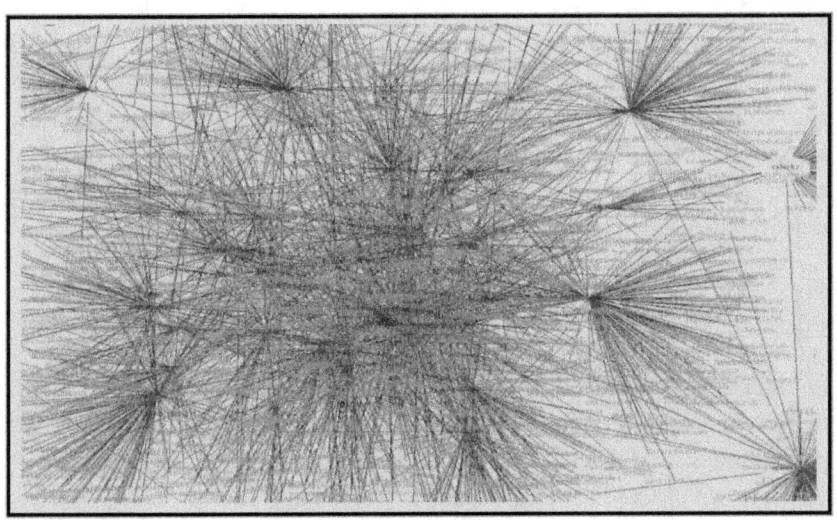

A Lot of *Something* on a Slide

The third situation is what might be considered the mortal mistake in slide use. In my opinion, the most egregious error is when a speaker *knows* that the material isn't legible to the audience because he or she has done a dry run of the presentation. It's clear to the speaker that the visuals aren't interpretable, but the deficiency is ignored. In such situations, the presenter, who I'll call "Speaker 3," unashamedly uttered to the audience: "I know that the information on this slide is too small to read, but . . ." In fact, the speaker was correct. No one could make sense of what was on the slide; Speaker 3 tried in vain to explain what it contained; and the audience was prevented from learning the important concept the speaker was trying to communicate.

As I sat in the audience for that presentation listening to the remarks of Speaker 3, a time came for audience questions at the end of the presentation. I struggled to restrain myself from asking, "If you knew the slides were impossible to read, then why did you include them anyway?"

Too much density on a slide is especially frustrating for listeners who *want* to engage with the presentation and to learn something from it. Cognitive scientists have discovered much about how our minds take in, process, and retain input such as that shown on a projected slide. A particular approach to learning called *information processing theory*[10] has provided many insights into the likely mechanisms and barriers to attention, motivation, recall and other important aspects of learning. It has also generated much practical advice such as considerations for how much input humans can attend to. The following sections will apply some of that advice in the form of principles that can be employed to avoid the epic fails experienced by Speakers 1, 2, and 3. In those cases and most others, the antidotes to density are piloting and parsimony.

Piloting

Speaker 2 had the right impulse: reviewing how the slides would look prior to presentation. Whenever a slide deck is used as part of a sermon, the exact presentation should get a trial run on the exact equipment and in the exact venue in which the slides will be used. Every time? Yes.

The piloting of a presentation can address many issues. For one, it can help with timing of the sermon. For another, a projected slide deck looks much different than it appears on one's laptop or desktop. A slide that is legible on a large monitor 24 inches away on one's desk may not be readable from 100 feet away for someone seated near the narthex. A dry run of the presentation also permits viewing the projected content from different parts of a sanctuary to aid in evaluating if the presentation will be accessible from different distances, angles, and elevations. Finally, if trial runs of planned slide presentations routinely reveal that too small of a font was used for text included on a slide, after a few such piloting experiences, that reality will have the positive effect of causing *a priori* use of larger fonts during initial development of the presentation, nipping textual density in the bud for the future.

In my own experience, I've come to believe that there is no such thing as a font that is too large. The use of a larger font necessarily means that a slide will not be overwhelmed with too much text, pictures, and animations (a good thing). It results in better visibility for all listeners/viewers (another good thing). It transitions the presenter from over-reliance on each slide to provide all of the intended message to the use of slides with just a few words that function as prompts regarding what will be presented orally

---

10. The origins of information processing theory trace to the late 1960s. The foundational work in this area was produced by Atkinson and Shiffrin, *Human Memory*.

(also good). An additional learning benefit is that slides containing only succinct words or statements are more memorable for listeners than long passages of textual material (a *really* good thing).

Parsimony

Experts in presentation design are unanimous regarding the #1 most common design misstep in creating a presentation: Too. Many. Words.

In our context, parsimony is the principle that anything that can be accomplished using the fewest words possible, should be. Maximize minimalism.

Some slides function primarily to prompt the speaker about what he or she has planned to say at a given juncture in the sermon. This can be done in just a few memorable words, a graphic, or other image that prompts the speaker's recall. Other slides function to provide listeners with structure to support cognitive incorporation of the information being presented. Such slides can be created as an outline, using bulleted points, or as any framework that aids listeners to organize the information to be stored.[11]

The field of instructional design has been informed by cognitive research on this point. Although there is still some theoretical discussion about the differences between short term memory and working memory, it is clear that all human viewers/listeners have a limited capacity with respect to incoming input. Research has suggested that the limits for an average person are around seven pieces or four chunks of information for processing,[12] further supporting the principle of parsimony that fewer is better.

I'll avoid getting into the weeds with how-to tips in this section, but I will commend readers interested in the development and use of slide presentation to some outstanding work that has been compiled by others. For example, presentation specialist and author of *slide:ology*, Nancy Duarte, has suggested some practical guidance to help discern when a slide

---

11. Robinson had some fairly harsh words regarding providing sermon outlines, saying: "We out not to put the outline on vulgar display" and that effective preaching involves "hiding the bones of a sermon," *Biblical Preaching*, 137. That advice predates much of what has been discovered about learning; giving listeners some framework for organizing what they hear is now universally regarded as beneficial to learning.

12. Additional information on the limits of working memory can be found in Miller, *The Magical Number Seven* and Cowan, *The Magical Number 4*.

contains too many words. Duarte has cleverly classified slide content into the three categories. According to her guidelines, a slide with more than 75 words is a document; a slide with 50 or so words functions essentially as a teleprompter for the speaker. Only slides with dramatically fewer words—or even just a few images—constitute a presentation.[13] An adaptation of Duarte's description of these three situations—and her recommendations for how to address them—are provided in Table 5-2.

Table 5-2
Three Categories of Slide Presentations

The Document	*The Teleprompter*	*The Presentation*
A slide of more than 75 words is a document. Revise the slide to reduce the amount of content on it, or just admit that it is a document and not a presentation. If it *is* a document, host a meeting instead. Circulate the document ahead of time or allow the audience to read it at the start.	A slide containing approximately 50 words is a teleprompter. This type of slide is often the result of insufficient time spent rehearsing the presentation. In order to read the slide, speakers typically must turn their backs to their audience. In most cases, the audience can read silently faster than the speaker can read aloud and must wait for the speaker to catch up.	A true presentation focuses on the big picture ideas and concepts the speaker intends to communicate. The slides reinforce the content with visuals, images, or key points rather than create distraction, allowing the audience to comfortably focus on both what is spoken and projected.

Producing parsimony in a slide presentation takes only modest effort, but some creating thinking. Figures 5-4 through 5-6 present a series of slides in which a gradual increase in parsimony is illustrated. For this hypothetical example, let us assume that a sermon was created to focus on key principles related to temptation. The homilist wanted to make three main points which, flowing from the speaker's initial attention to parsimony, were distilled to be expressed as succinctly as possible with supporting Scripture references in a first draft of the slide presentation:

13. A common practical recommendation for slide density is referred to as the 6 x 6 Rule: the number of lines on a slide should be not exceed 6, and there should be no more than 6 words per line.

Vehicles

1) We should be ever alert to temptation and not surprised by trials because Scripture indicates that we are lured into sin by our own desires and enticed by Satan. ("Beloved, do not be surprised at the fiery trial when it comes upon you to test you, as though something strange were happening to you." I Peter 4:12, ESV)

2) Giving in to temptation feeds the flesh, but the flesh is never satisfied by feeding it. ("Just as Death and Destruction are never satisfied, so human desire is never satisfied." Proverbs 27:20)

3) God has promised that he is our helper—not the source of temptation, but of escape from it. ("And God is faithful; he will not let you be tempted beyond what you can bear. But when you are tempted, he will also provide a way out so that you can endure it." (I Corinthians 10:13b NIV)

Figure 5-4 shows a slide with just those three main points and the key supporting Scripture reference for each. Most readers will immediately observe that rather than including all three points on one slide, it would be less dense if three separate slides were used. Fair enough, although slides such as the one shown in Figure 5-4 are surprisingly common. Other than density of text, there are other features of the first iteration that detract from its potential to aid learners in grasping and retaining its content. For one, the background of the slide makes it difficult to read. What must have seemed to be an innocuous background template because of its simplicity—especially compared to other, much busier background options that are available—actually detracts from the ability to read the slide's content. The fact that the margins of the slide had to be adjusted and a small font size had to be used accommodate all of the text is another clue that there is just too much there.[14] Finally—and I'll make no recommendations for specific font choices here, only an observation—some fonts are substantially easier to read than others. The font used in this case (probably the default font on many word processing programs, Times New Roman) is distinguished by its use of serifs—those slight, flourishing strokes at the edges of each character and used in many other fonts. Such fonts are generally discouraged for presentations and sans-serif fonts are preferred.

---

14. Presentation specialists recommend that a font no smaller than 24 be used for presentations, with preference for "the larger, the better."

Figure 5-5 shows an alternative version of the same content covered in the first slide, but with greater attention to parsimony. The full Scripture quotations have been trimmed to just their references, which the speaker can still rely on as prompts to read the relevant references separately as appropriate. Because there is now less crowding on the slide, the margins have been adjusted, making the slide appear much less cluttered. A cleaner background has been used. A sans-serif font has been substituted.

A penultimate version of the slide showing a second iteration in parsimony is provided in Figure 5-6. This version shows a dramatic reduction in material contained on the slide, while still prompting the speaker regarding the three key points to be made—and in a manner so succinct that viewers of the slide are more likely to be able to recall them. We'll return to the three main points of this sermon and a look at what a final version illustrating parsimonious presentation might look like in the following "Images" section of this chapter.

Figure 5-4

> **Three Principles of Temptation**
>
> 1) We should be ever alert to temptation and not surprised by trials because Scripture indicates that we are lured into sin by our own desires and enticed by Satan. ("Beloved, do not be surprised at the fiery trial when it comes upon you to test you, as though something strange were happening to you." 1 Peter 4:12, ESV)
>
> 2) Giving in to temptation feeds the flesh, but the flesh is never satisfied by feeding it. ("Just as Death and Destruction are never satisfied, so human desire is never satisfied." Proverbs 27:20 NLT)
>
> 3) God has promised that he is our helper—not the source of temptation, but of escape from it. ("And God is faithful; he will not let you be tempted beyond what you can bear. But when you are tempted, he will also provide a way out so that you can endure it." 1 Corinthians 10:13b NIV)

Lack of Parsimony in Slide Content

Figure 5-5

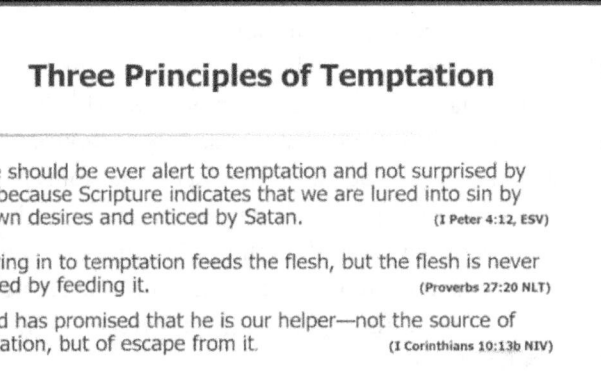

Improvement 1 in Slide Parsimony

Figure 5-6

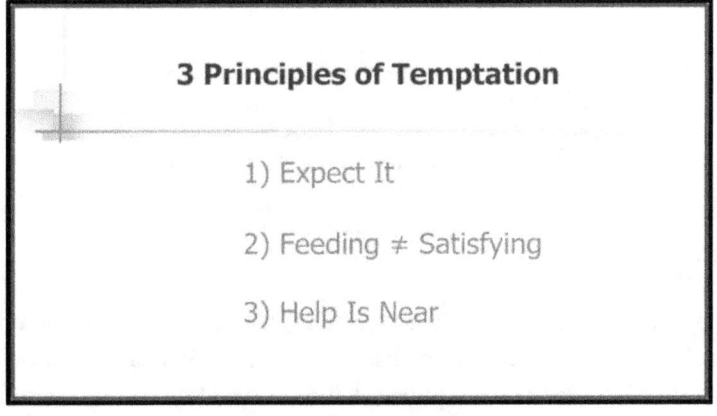

Improvement 2 in Slide Parsimony

Figures 5-7 and 5-8 provide another illustration of parsimony in a slide presentation, taken from an actual sermon. In that sermon, the speaker contrasted the nature of God's design for government as evident at the time of the creation, with how the design and implications of government have changed in contemporary times. The presentation consisted of single words, linked with arrows, and a building of the sermon as each new aspect of the two designs was introduced. As can be seen in Figure 5-7, the first slide (which showed just the two headings, "Creation" and "Modernity") was used to introduce the topic of the sermon. The second slide provided two additional words to prompt elaboration of the point that creation was organized as an aspect of God's morality.

Figure 5-8 shows the final slide and the full sermon organization. The main ideas (i.e., that, as created, governments were instituted to adopt laws based on God's morality, and that, modernity has reversed the situation, whereby governments adopt laws that define morality) were developed point-by-point as each arrow and single word were introduced sequentially. In this way, the single final slide shown in Figure 5-8 presented the full sermon in a way that aided both the speaker in structuring and delivering the sermon and, importantly, it aided the congregation in seeing, organizing, and recalling them.

Figure 5-7

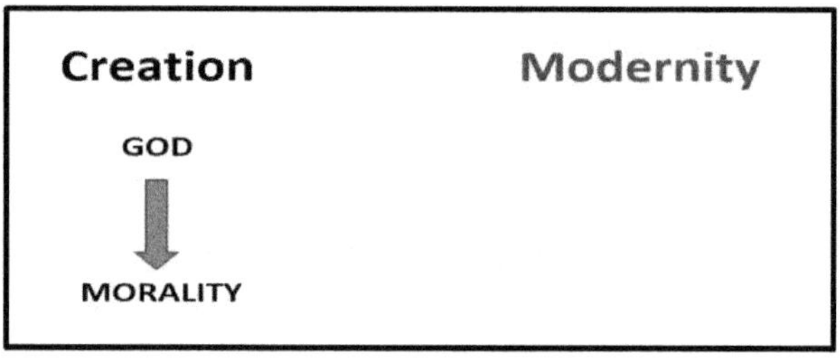

Creation   **Modernity**

GOD

⬇

MORALITY

Using Projected Text to Structure a Sermon

Reading

Perhaps the most ineffective use of a slide deck occurs when the content of the slides is simply read to the listeners. In the worst case, reading slides to sermon listeners creates a physical and personal disconnect with them, as the speaker typically must turn his or her back to the audience to read them. As was addressed in Chapter 3, time is also lost, as listeners can visually process a slide much more quickly than it takes the speaker to read it to them; in those situations, there is the awkwardness of waiting for the speaker to catch up. In addition—and regardless of whether it is true or not—reading slides to a congregation can signal that the speaker did not spend an adequate amount of time preparing and rehearsing what would be covered by the sermon. Finally, although hearing and viewing modalities can be complementary and aid learning, what is spoken and what is projected can also compete for listeners' attention.

Figure 5-8

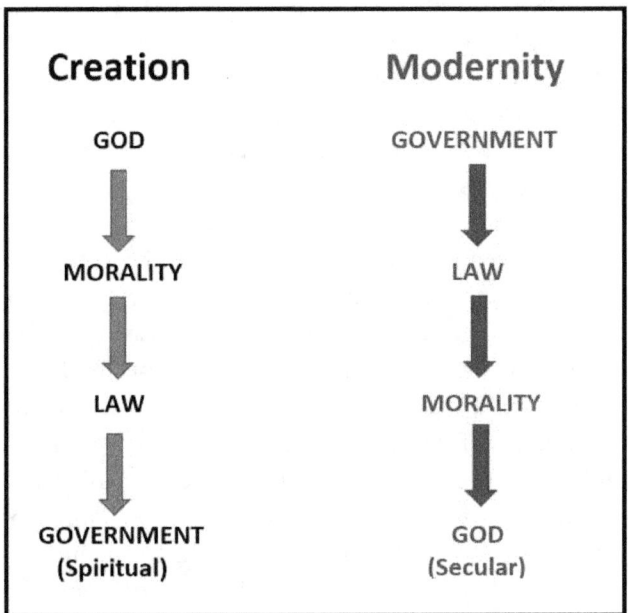

Using Projected Text to Structure a Sermon

The presentation specialist cited previously, Nancy Duarte, has put the matter succinctly: "The audience will either read your slides or listen to you. They will not do both."[15] She recommends that, in every instance where text is to be presented to an audience, the speaker should ask if it is more important that they listen (implying that minimal, if any, accompanying text should be presented on a slide) or if it is more effective if the audience reads some specific material (implying that the speaker should allocate appropriate an amount of time for them to do so).

Animation

Just as spoken and visual information can compete for listeners' attention, so too can other features of a slide deck presentation such as the ubiquitous animations, transitions, and other special attention-seeking effects. A key principle in the learning sciences is what has been called the *cognitive load*

---

15. Quotation retrieved from www.amazon.com/slide-ology-Science-Creating-Presentations/dp/0596522347

of a task (such as processing the information presented in a sermon). Cognitive load refers to the amount of a person's working memory resources that are required to effectively process information. When preparing a sermon, consideration should be given to ensuring the cognitive load on listeners is not unnecessarily burdensome.

Current theory related to the mental demands of learning postulates that there are three types of cognitive load:

Intrinsic. Intrinsic cognitive load refers to the the cognitive demands associated with a specific topic. Simply put, intrinsic cognitive load is how hard the material is to learn. The cognitive demands associated with a topic about which listeners are familiar would be modest; the load associated with an unfamiliar topic could be substantial. For example, there might be little cognitive load for listeners in a sermon dealing with how to meet the food and shelter needs of families from a local neighborhood where a recent fire destroyed their homes. Greater cognitive load might be involved for listeners to a sermon on the challenges and linguistic nuances faced by missionaries attempting to translate the Bible into the language with no written alphabet.

Germane. Germane cognitive load refers to the mental work of moving information back and forth between working memory and more permanent memory storage and of creating connections between new information and information already stored in long term memory. Even when the intrinsic cognitive load is light, cognitive resources are used to engage in the information processing task.

Extraneous. Extraneous cognitive load refers to the way in which information is presented to a learner; it is the extra mental "work" that listeners must perform to differentiate between input that is not directly relevant to the information that is intended to be learned and the information that is relevant. A useful analogy here is that of listening to music while riding in a car and the concept of the signal-to-noise ratio in engineering. In this situation, noise (e.g., traffic sounds, static on the radio, poor satellite reception) comprises the elements that make the can make the signal (i.e., the music) difficult to hear. When the signal-to-noise ratio is large, the music comes through loud and clear; when it is small, distractions abound, and additional effort is required to focus on listening to it.

Contemporary research on and applications of the concept of cognitive load were influenced by research begun in the late 1980s by Australian cognitive psychologist John Sweller. Sweller argued that intentional instructional design strategies should be used to reduce cognitive load for learners—especially sources of cognitive load that are irrelevant to the intended message. Such "unburdening" can foster more efficient and more effective learning.[16]

Reducing extraneous cognitive load—that is, reducing noise and enhancing the signal—has clear relevance for creating effective slide deck presentations that accompany sermons. What constitutes extraneous cognitive load in a slide presentation? Among other things: audio sound effects, visual effects, slide changes, backgrounds, slide animations, and so on—in short, anything not related to the actual content of the presentation.

How do these extraneous aspects of a presentation affect cognitive load? According to cognitive scientists, they compete for the listeners' attention with the intended message; that is, with the burdens inherent in the intrinsic and germane cognitive loading. The extraneous aspects require listeners to allocate cognitive resources to sift through and dismiss some elements of a presentation (or be distracted by them) so that the relevant information can be contemplated, processed, and—ideally—encoded into long term memory for later use when applicable. However, our cognitive processing resources are finite; during any presentation, we all subconsciously allocate those finite resources to identifying and discounting less relevant input such as visual effects, animations, and so on while simultaneously identifying and processing the content of the presentation. Three principles follow from this:

1) the greater the allocation of cognitive resources demanded by extraneous elements, the fewer resources listeners will have available for the intrinsic and germane elements;

2) the more dense a presentation is in terms of either kind of input (i.e., density of content or density of the audio/visual features of the slide presentation itself), the more taxing it is for listeners to do the cognitive sifting required and to process the information in such a way as to be most memorable and useful; and, therefore,

---

16. See Sweller, *Cognitive Load During Problem Solving*.

3) every slide deck should be scrutinized to ensure that whatever features are incorporated serve to focus listeners on and enhance access to the content of the sermon and do not needlessly distract from the intended message.

An Addendum on Parsimony

As a segue to the next section on the use of images, I'll now return to the slide presentation described previously designed to accompany a sermon covering three key principles related to temptation:

1) we should be ever alert to temptation and not surprised that we encounter trials;
2) giving in to temptation feeds the flesh, but the flesh is never satisfied by feeding it; and
3) God has promised that He will be our help in times of temptation.

As an uber-parsimonious iteration of the slide introduced in Figure 5-6, a speaker might opt to forego text entirely in favor of using images. Figure 5-9 shows a hypothetical way in which the three points above might be represented as visual images instead of text. The pair of eyes, the sweet-tooth craving for cake, and the racing ambulance provide highly efficient cues to aid the speaker's recall of the three main points he or she planned to address regarding vigilance, feeding the flesh, and God's promise of help. Equally important, the three images provide a potent encoding adjunct for listeners to the spoken sermon to aid in their recall of those points. We now turn to a more focused examination of images and the powerful recall and encoding aid they can offer.

VEHICLES

Figure 5-9

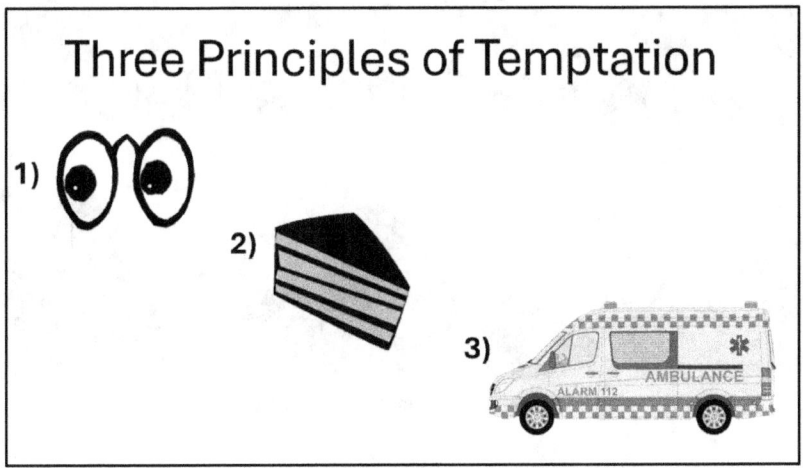

Using Images to Increase Parsimony

IMAGES

In Chapter 2, we saw that people's ability to remember and use information can be affected by how the information was learned in the first place. Recall, for example, how seeing a vintage automobile might elicit memories of a high school prom or how a friend's remark in conversation somehow might bring to mind a favorite childhood television show. In the fields of cognitive science and instructional design, such phenomenon are examples of what is called *encoding*—the cognitive process of packaging information for storage and later retrieval. According to that perspective, the high school prom memory was suddenly evoked years later upon seeing a 1976 Volkswagen Karmann Ghia like that shown in Figure 5-10 (the same kind of vehicle that drove a group of friends to the high school event) and the friend's comments about the Houston, Texas major league baseball team—the Astros—included the word that the cartoon family, the Jetsons (see Figure 5-11), chose for their family pet. Hearing or seeing one bit of information in the present brought back to consciousness other similar or related information from the past that had previously been stored in long term memory.

Figure 5-10

1976 Volkswagen Karmann Ghia

Figure 5-11

The Jetsons Cartoon Family with Pet, Astro

At some time in the present, auditory, olfactory, gustatory, and even tactile sensations may serve as the input that triggers recall of long-distant information that was originally encoded along with input to those senses. Among the most effective triggers for recall is visual input.

Vehicles

By visual input, I am *not* referring to the text-based information just considered that comprises the visual elements of a slide presentation. What I *am* referring to are visual images, graphics, icons, pictures, symbols, or other simple visuals that can be powerful aids to recollection and application. If it is true that pictures are worth a thousand words, they have even greater value for securing memory of associated input and evoking recall of that information.

The cognitive science underlying the inclusion of visual stimuli is well established. In fact, at least one researcher has provided evidence that visual stimuli—that is, images, not just projected words on a screen—are more efficacious than text in stimulating recall. To illustrate this, let us imagine for example the differential effect produced by a speaker saying, "Wouldn't it be frightening to see a shark fin skimming along the surface of a body of water?" compared to projecting the image shown in Figure 5-12 accompanied by an audio excerpt of the theme from the movie *Jaws*.

Figure 5-12

Shark Fin

William Hockley, a professor at Wilfrid Laurier University in Ontario, Canada has investigated what he has termed the *picture superiority effect* and documented that pictures and and other non-text images are more likely to be remembered than words.[17] The work of another Canadian scholar sug-

17. Hockley, *The Picture Superiority Effect*.

gested that the use of words *and* pictures may have a combination effect. A faculty member at the University of Western Ontario, Allan Paivio conducted research on what has been called *dual coding theory*.[18] According to dual coding theory, there are two ways a person stores (and recalls) learned material: verbal information and images. Although he postulated people process and store imagery and verbal information differently, both imagery and verbal information are used for recall. Perhaps the most relevant summary of Paivio's work is that the ability to encode potential new learning in two different ways increases the chance of remembering the information versus presentation in only one way.

Two applications of dual coding theory come readily to mind from sermons I've attended. In both examples, a visual presented with the spoken words of the sermon helped me to learn, retain, and recall the essential points of the sermons. The following two examples might prompt readers to think of similar examples in their own background.

The first example is drawn from a sermon I heard on racial injustice. At some point in the sermon, the speaker described the work of William Wilberforce. Wilberforce (1759-1833) was a member of the British Parliament and leader of the movement to abolish the slave trade in England. He was the driving force behind the Slave Trade Act of 1807 which, although it did not abolish slavery in the UK, did prohibit the slave trade across the British Empire. His efforts are also credited with the eventual passage of the Slavery Abolition Act of 1833 which effectively abolished slavery across the Empire, and which was passed just one month after Wilberforce died.

I had heard of Wilberforce prior to hearing the sermon, but I had only a minimal recollection of him as a historical figure, a vague sense of his Christian faith, and no specific recall of his abolitionist fervor despite the fact that, at some time previously, I had read his classic work, *Real Christianity*.[19] During the sermon and in the course of discussing Wilberforce's pursuit of abolition, the speaker also showed a picture of Wilberforce (see Figure 5-13). Although the manner of Wilberforce's dress in the picture blurred in with that of many such historical figures of the Revolutionary War period in the United States, for some reason—I now suspect dual coding theory—the key points of the sermon have not blurred in my mind.

18. Paivio, *Imagery and Verbal Processes*, and Paivio, *Mental Representations*.

19. Wilberforce, *Real Christianity*. The 1982 edition is an updated version of Wilberforce's original treatise published in 1797 and bearing the longer but more descriptive title, *A Practical View of the Prevailing Religious System of Professed Christians in the Higher and Middle Classes in This Country Contrasted with Real Christianity*.

Since that time, I have had a clear and detailed recollection of not only Wilberforce's work, but also greater sensitivity regarding how professing Christians can be blind to issues of social injustice since hearing and viewing that presentation.

Figure 5-13

William Wilberforce, Portrait by Karl Anton Hickel, 1794

The second example from my own experiences involves the unusual case of a Christian man bestowed sainthood by the Catholic church. I would have never imagined there would be someone canonized as the patron saint of ugly people, although that is indeed how the person celebrated on April 16, St. Drogo the Shepherd, is known.[20] Drogo (1105-1186), shown in Figure 5-14, was born in Epinoy, Flanders and worked as a shepherd early in

20. Although best known as the patron saint of unattractive people, Drogo is also thought of as a source of comfort to those with broken bones, hernias, kidney stones, the mentally ill, deaf people, cattle, shepherds, orphans, expectant mothers, the sick, and coffee house keepers. See https://anastpaul.com/2019/04/16/saint-of-the-day-16-april-saint-drogo-1105-1186

his life. He went on several pilgrimages to Rome. He apparently contracted a disease on one pilgrimage that left him severely deformed. Subsequently, he resigned to a reclusive life of prayer and fasting, living in a small cell attached to a church in Sebourg, France, where he remained for over 40 years until his death. The homily I heard on unconditional love for those we encounter regardless of their outward appearances—accompanied by the image of St. Drogo—forever cemented that essential sermon point in my mind.

Figure 5-14

Statue of St. Drogo of Sebourg

I could provide dozens of other more contemporary examples, ranging from images I've seen of comedian/inspirational speaker Nick Vujicic who was born without limbs, to author Joni Eareckson Tada who became disabled at an early age due to a diving accident, and Luther College football player Chris Norton, who was injured in a collegiate football game. In each case, very powerful images seen in a YouTube video of Nick Vujicic,[21]

21. Vujicic, *Nothing is Impossible*.

a book cover image of Joni Eareckson Tada,[22] and a Netflix movie titled *7 Yards: The Chris Norton Story*[23] combined with a text-based or verbal message that was being communicated to make my recall of that message more impactful and longer lasting.

As a final example of the power of images, however, I would point to the Super Bowl advertising campaign, "He Gets Us," that has been prominent in recent years. It is not known exactly how much it cost to purchase the 60-second spot shown for Super Bowl LVII, but it has been reported that 30-second ads for Super Bowl LVIII are going for $7 million. The 2024 ad featured various foot washing scenes intended to communicate Christians' responsibility to love our neighbors. The ad consisted of essentially no text; it simply contained a series of still images depicting one person washing the foot of another.[24] I can't imagine any more compelling evidence of the power of images than represented by the fact that an advertiser would spend over $10 million to present images for 60 seconds.[25]

STORIES

Even though we're now fully immersed in a digital, or even post-digital age in which technologies such as streaming video, computer-generated imagery, marketing tailored to personal web usage behavior, and artificial intelligence renderings of images and voices are ever-present, stories remain a legacy technology of sorts that has not lost its power. Years ago, Robinson noted that ". . . whatever else the Bible is, it is a storybook. Old Testament theology comes packaged in narratives . . ."[26] A contemporary commentator on social trends described the expansive power of narratives in this way:

> "Stories possess a unique ability to impact our psychology. They engage our emotions, creating connections and fostering empathy with characters and their experiences. Research has shown that storytelling activates various regions of the brain, enhancing memory retention and recall. By stimulating our senses and

22. Eareckson, *Joni*.

23. *7 Yards: The Chris Norton Story*.

24. Examples of these images can be viewed at https://hegetsus.com/en/articles/foot-washing-image-gallery

25. See https://www.sportingnews.com/us/nfl/news/super-bowl-ad-he-gets-us-jesus-commercial-explained/1fa7ad9d2b009aad27bbce80

26. Robinson, *Biblical Preaching*, 124.

emotions, narratives leave a lasting imprint on our minds, shaping our beliefs, attitudes, and behaviors . . . Cultural narratives play a crucial role in the formation of individual and collective identities. Myths, legends, and folklore passed down through generations contribute to shaping cultural values, traditions, and worldviews. These narratives provide a sense of belonging, reinforcing shared beliefs and strengthening social bonds."[27]

The power of narratives has been explored in the context of homiletics, largely in the 1970s. In a festschrift for Thomas Long, Alyce McKenzie observes that the "New Homiletic" paradigm "was undergirded by the conviction that people are inherently story-makers, that we are all engaged in the process of making a coherent narrative out of the disjointed events of our daily lives."[28] Stephen Crites, in his essay on "The Narrative Quality of Experience" argued that "storytelling [is] one of the most important cultural expressions" and that "the formal quality of experience through time is inherently narrative."[29]

In my own academic work, I have examined the role of narratives in education, particularly the way in which they have become the *lingua franca* of practicing teachers[30] for describing their teaching methods to others. I have also written about how stories have become a mainstream way of reporting research findings.[31] As noted above, narratives have a remarkable pervasiveness, permanence, and potency.

In the context of sermons, a memorable story—real or contrived—can be a forceful factor to aid listeners in remembering a main point. Here are two examples drawn from my experience listening to sermons that illustrate the power of stories. The first is a story from the real-life experience of Dr. Scott Gibson; the second is a fictitious account of an aspiring corporate ladder climber.

Gibson delivered a sermon at the Truett Theological Seminary in Waco, Texas, in which he argued for urgency in sharing the Gospel with others.[32] The poignant story he related from his days pastoring a small

---

27. Jefferey, *The Power of Storytelling*. For a more comprehensive, scholarly examination, see Gregory, *Shaped by Stories*.

28. McKenzie, "Form Follows Function," 21.

29. Crites, "The Narrative Quality of Experience," 291.

30. Cizek, *The Tale Wagging the Dog: Narrative and Neo-Pragmatism*.

31. Cizek, *The Hegemony of the Narrative*.

32. Gibson, *Tall Orders*.

Appalachian congregation imprinted that sermon's main message on all his listeners. The story revolved around the death of a man named E. C. Bailey. Gibson described Bailey as an elderly, kind-hearted, but alcoholic non-believer who had befriended an aging, disabled, homebound member of his congregation named Polly. Polly contacted her pastor, Rev. Gibson to ask him to visit E. C. who had been admitted to a rural hospital about 30 miles away. Gibson found E. C. dying of heart failure, struggling to breathe, on the edge of eternity. In his last breath, E. C. responded affirmatively to Gibson's invitation to come to faith in Jesus, ask forgiveness of his sins, and accept God's gift of everlasting life. It was a vivid narrative about a life transformed and it drove home his points about the urgency of sharing the Gospel in a world where we often can't know God's timing for the lives of those with whom we interact.

The fictitious narrative example is one for which I am unable to recall when I first heard it, though it was surely 25 years ago or more. That alone attests to the staying power of stories. Importantly, I not only recall the story (and I have retold it many times since), but also the principle it was intended to help me learn.

The story concerns a junior executive, new to a very large company, who hoped to gain the knowledge, wisdom, and insights that might facilitate his rapid ascendance up the corporate ladder. He knew by reputation that the current CEO of the company had accomplished a successful rise to power and prominence, and he wished to do the same. On of his strategies for doing so was to probe the CEO for what accounted for his success.

The young executive contacted the CEO's administrative assistant to inquire about the possibility of scheduling an appointment for a one-on-one meeting with the CEO. He was discouraged to learn of the CEO's busy schedule, and that the first opening for such a chat would be a modest 15-minute appointment six months down the road. He made the appointment.

With the passage of the six-month wait, the time finally arrived for the young executive's precious 15-minute meeting with the CEO. Taking the elevator to the C-suite on the 42nd floor, he wasted little time with sociolinguistic niceties and got right to the question on his mind:

> Young Executive: *"Thank you for your time today, sir. I really appreciate how busy you are and how little time we have, so excuse me if I jump right to a question I've really been wanting to hear your thoughts about."*

CEO: *"Go right ahead."*

Young Executive: *"Well, sir, obviously you have been very successful, and I'd like to learn from your experience. Can you tell me any secrets to your success? To what do you attribute how you have risen to your position of leadership in such a large and influential company?"*

The CEO paused for a few moments, rubbed his chin pensively, the finally answered: *"Hmmm . . . I suppose I'd have to say that any success I've had is the result of many, many good decisions."*

The Young Executive internally evaluated that response as obvious and not very helpful, so he followed up: *"That's pretty clear, sir, but if I may: What's the key to making those many, many good decisions?"*

CEO: *"Many, many bad decisions."*

The sermon in which that narrative was embedded had as its main points the trials we encounter in the Christian life, how we grow as Christians, and the positive effect that even adverse events have the potential to make in our lives. The sermon centered on the familiar Scripture from the fifth chapter of Romans:

> *We can rejoice, too, when we run into problems and trials, for we know that they help us develop endurance. And endurance develops strength of character, and character strengthens our confident hope of salvation. And this hope will not lead to disappointment.*[33]

The CEO had grown in wisdom, patience, and character via the problems he had faced early on, gaining insight, persistence, and confidence for how he handled subsequent challenges. The Scripture and the memorable illustrative story provided a template for how believers should view our present sufferings—and emphasizing that we must not only endure but learn from them. Narratives such as these can as powerful and memorable—or more so—than any slide deck or technological accoutrement in helping listeners to grasp, recall, and use the main point of a sermon.

EXAMPLES

The final vehicle for aiding listeners to learn from a sermon is the use of examples. In the learning sciences, examples have been an area of extensive research. Among other things, scholars have studied how examples

---

33. Romans 5: 3-5a

function in the learning process,[34] what makes a good example,[35] optimal arrangement and sequencing of examples during instruction,[36] and differences in the examples chosen by novice and master teachers. Most of the research on examples has been carried out in what, for many readers, is probably the most challenging subject area: Math. Uhhhgggh. In my background work for this book, I learned that mathematicians even held a special conference devoted exclusively to "exemplification" at Oxford University in 2005.[37] The extensive research attention to examples suggests that they are important for meaningful learning to occur.

But *why* is the use of examples so important? There are two reasons. First, research in the area of instructional design has long affirmed the incorporation of many, diverse examples as important for facilitating learning, comprehension, and application of concepts, particularly challenging concepts. The more challenging the concept, the greater quantity and diversity of examples are needed. Certainly, the Scriptures are replete with concepts that can be difficult to understand and apply:

- What does loving my enemies look like?[38]
- How can I keep the Sabbath holy?[39]
- How is it possible to pray continually?[40]
- What does it mean that I should I be as shrewd as a snake?[41]
- What does it look like to hate my father and mother, wife and children, brothers and sisters . . ?[42]

---

34. See Reimann and Schult, "Turning Examples into Cases" and Rissland, "Example-based Reasoning."

35. See Atkinson, Derry, Renkl, and Wortham, "Learning from Examples;" and Goldenberg, "What Constitutes a Good Example?"

36. See Tennyson and Park, "The Teaching of Concepts," and Petty and Jansson, "Sequencing Examples and Non-examples."

37. A small group of mathematics educators gathered for three days in June 2005 in Oxford, England around the topic of exemplification. A paper by Bills, et al. "*Exemplification in Mathematics Education*," provides an overview of the conference.

38. Matthew 5:44a

39. Exodus 20:8

40. 1 Thessalonians 5:17 (NIV)

41. Matthew 10:16b

42. Luke 14:26

- How would someone blaspheme against the Holy Spirit?[43]
- How is it possible to be perfect, even our heavenly Father is perfect?[44]

These Scriptures and many others cry out for examples to illuminate their meaning.

Second, the use of examples aids listeners who are learning a concept to apply that concept in their own lives. In the survey of Catholic parishioners cited in Chapter 2, respondents indicated that the strongest predictor of a sermon's impact was its perceived relevance to their lives.[45]

The technical term for the described the ability to use what has been learned in one context in new contexts is called *transfer*.[46] Research on transfer goes back to at least the turn of the previous century.[47] The potential for transfer is essential to consider in considering inclusion of examples to illustrate key points: even if a Biblical principle is comprehensively expounded in a sermon and grasped by listeners, it may never be available for them to apply in their daily lives if it's not clear how to do so.

Transfer is complicated because each of us have differing backgrounds and circumstances, and we encounter diverse situations in which something we learn might be applied. The more a sermon can illustrate how the Biblical concept applies using examples that are as close as possible to the backgrounds, circumstances, and situations of the listeners, the greater potential impact the new learning will have.

NON-EXAMPLES

Following the strong consensus regarding the value of examples for learning, I have tried to incorporate many concrete examples, illustrations, and analogies in this book. I have also tried to incorporate another best practice found to be highly effective in certain situations—the use of *non-examples* to accompany examples as a means of clarifying what is intended to be learned about the overarching concept. Just as the characteristics of good

---

43. Matthew 12:31

44. Matthew 5:48

45. Pargament and Silverman, "Exploring Some Correlates of Sermon Impact on Catholic Parishioners."

46. National Research Council, *How People Learn*.

47. Woodworth and Thorndike, "The Influence of Improvement in One Mental Function."

examples have been studied by researchers in the field of instructional design, the characteristics of effective non-examples have been studied as well.[48] The pairing of an example with a non-example related to the same concept is often particularly effective in learning.

Non-examples should be considered for inclusion in a sermon whenever it is critical to help clarify not only what a concept is but what it is *not*; what a Scripture means and what it doesn't; when a principle should be applied and when it shouldn't. Here's an example of pairing an example with a non-example: In medical school, aspiring pediatricians learn not only what a young child should be given when experiencing flu-like symptoms (e.g., plenty of fluids, acetaminophen or ibuprofen, and lighter, breathable clothing), but also what the child should *not* be given—specifically aspirin, which has been associated with the life-threatening condition knows as Reyes Syndrome. "Do this; *don't* do that."

In a similar way, in some situations it is important to communicate in a sermon what should not be done. A story from chapter 2 of the book of Job provides a clear illustration. Job's three friends Eliphaz, Bildad, are Zophar are often put forward as an example of what should be done when a friend is suffering: they immediately came to be with Job;[49] they empathized with Job when they saw first-hand his afflictions;[50] and they gave a substantial amount of their time (seven days) to supporting their friend.[51] A colleague of mine, James Huegerich, who worked as a crisis intervention specialist for a police department in North Carolina, related how he simplified these three elements in his approach to dealing with citizens affected by a crisis situation: His operating principle is to "Show up, shut up, and send up [prayer]."

An important caveat is also sometimes mentioned related to the events during Job's time of crisis. At least initially, the three friends simply sat in silence with Job, mourning with him; they didn't offer any input, critique,

---

48. See Tennyson, Woolley, and Merrill, "Exemplar and Non-exemplar Variables," and Peled Zaslavsky, "Counter-Examples that (Only) Prove and Counter-examples that (also) Explain."

49. "When three of Job's friends heard of the tragedy he had suffered, they got together and traveled from their homes to comfort and console him." (Job 2:11)

50. "When they saw Job from a distance, they scarcely recognized him. Wailing loudly, they tore their robes and threw dust into the air over their heads to show their grief" (Job 2:12).

51. "Then they sat on the ground with him for seven days and nights" (Job 2:13a).

or suggestions.[52] That leads to the non-example. The subsequent actions of Eliphaz, Bildad, are Zophar provide practical non-examples—what *not* to do when someone is facing a difficult situation. The three would have been remembered as faithful companions had they not digressed into the long-winded diatribes chronicled in chapters 4-25 that included accusations, assertions, and advice that effectively negated any support they had provided. God and Job are unanimous in condemning the actions of the three friends and those actions are held up as non-examples.[53]

A Word of Caution about Examples

I have had some bad experiences with examples. Over approximately 35 years of teaching two courses each semester, student evaluations of my teaching have been strong and faculty colleagues who have observed my teaching have been uniformly positive. My teaching today is better than it was 35 years ago; I suspect that is due in large part to the fact that, like the CEO in the example earlier in this chapter, I have made some very, very bad decisions.

Here's one.

First, in some situations, I have found it imperative *not* to provide an example. This is not really something that learning scientists have discovered, but something I discovered from personal experience. One particular experience sticks in my mind. As background, I have great difficulty in remembering people's names. I don't know why. I've tried a lot of different tricks that sales and marketing people might recommend to help me with that difficulty. For example, I've tried forming a mental image when meeting someone to associate with their name and help recall. If I were to meet a very tall, thin person named Jerry, I might think of a giraffe. Jerry=Giraffe. No help: when I see the person again, all I can remember is "giraffe" not his name. It's sometimes recommended to repeat the person's name several times when first meeting them. "Oh, hello, Phoebe." "It's nice to meet you, Phoebe." "That's a great scarf, Phoebe." "How long have you worked here,

---

52. "No one said a word to Job, for they saw that his suffering was too great for words" (Job 2:13b).

53. As recorded in Job chapter 42, verse 7, God says, "I am angry with you [Eliphaz] and your two friends, because you have not spoken the truth about me" and Job says to his friends, "You are miserable comforters, all of you!" (Job 16:2, NIV)

Phoebe?" The next time I ran into Phoebe even just a few days later, I still couldn't remember her name. I think all that technique accomplished was to leave Phoebe with the impression that I was annoying and should be avoided.

Each semester at the University of North Carolina, I typically have to learn the names of the new students in my courses. That's about 25 or so new names to learn each time. One of the other techniques I've actually used to some positive effect has been, in the first class meeting, having each student write their name on a 3" x 5" index card along with other important information such as a phone number and email address where they can be contacted. I then take time in that first meeting to go through the cards, meet each student, and get to know them a bit. At each subsequent class meeting, I arrive to class early; I bring the pile of cards to class; and I try to associate a name from the cards with each student as they enter the room before class begins.

When I first ask students to fill out the cards at that first class meeting, I give directions about how to write down their name: "Please write the name that you would like me to remember you by. That is, I know the university might have an 'official' name for you on file, but if you prefer to be called something else, please write down that name."

Here's where I learned *not* to use an example. At the beginning of one semester, I followed up on the directions with a specific example: ". . .but if you prefer to be called something else, please write down that name. For example, if your name is something stupid like 'Rudolph', and you prefer to be called 'Rudy' then just write 'Rudy' on your card."

I'm sure you can see where this is headed, and it isn't good. I chose as my example the name "Rudolph" because I figured there was no way someone in the class would have that name. Wrong. As I was reading each card out loud to get to know the students, I came across the card shown in Figure 5-15. I've redacted some of the personal identifying information on the card, but my mistake was obvious. I immediately regretted using the word "stupid" to characterize a name. I was even more mortified when I read what the student had written on his card. I apologized profusely to him and pressed on meeting the other students, but the shame I felt for the hurt I likely caused to Rudy made me just want to slink out of the classroom and never return.

Sermon Science

Figure 5-15

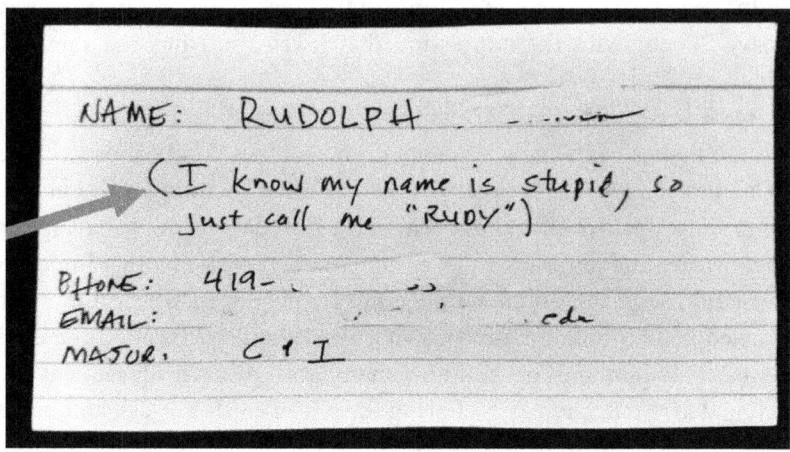

When an Example is *Not* a Good Idea

Another example is from a time my wife alerted me to when an example might not have been a good idea. During a church service one Sunday, the pastor wanted to recognize the important roles that different people play in our lives. As an example, he cited the role of mothers, and he asked all the mothers in the congregation to stand up so that they might be acknowledged. I thought that was a kind way of showing appreciation. My wife helped me see that the example may have been well received by most, but was also likely hurtful to some—for example, to women unable to have a child, to men, women, or children whose mother may have passed away recently, to those who had never known their mother, and so on.

In summary, four principles about the use of examples have been shown to help learning (or avoid hurt!) and should be considered in sermon development:

1) incorporate examples

2) incorporate non-examples in appropriate situations

3) prioritize examples that promote transfer and application

4) be sensitive to listeners when choosing examples

AN EMERGING CAUTION

Throughout this book, I've highlighted many positive aspects that research in the learning sciences can contribute to the efficacy of sermon development and delivery. Without question, technological advances have made sermon messages more engaging, accessible, and relevant to diverse audiences. However, it's not only preachers that incorporate technology: congregants have a number of technological tools at their disposal. At some risk of being labeled as unrealistic, I'll mention one technology—the smart phone—and describe an emerging research finding that should be considered.

Clearly, cell phones are ubiquitous in any congregation. They are useful tools for looking up an unknown word or obtaining a translation, following along with the reading of a Scripture passage during a sermon, or checking one's calendar for availability to attend an upcoming event announced at the end of a service. Although they may not use it—in fact, an announcement is sometimes made to put cell phones in quiet mode—in any congregation, it is certain that the vast majority of attendees will have a cell phone in their possession throughout the service.

Learning scientists have begun to study the effects of cell phones on attention and cognitive processing—the ability of listeners to think about what they are hearing. Obviously, placing bets on Draft Kings for the Monday night football game, checking one's 401(k) performance, texting family members about Sunday afternoon plans, swiping left on Tinder, or any other of a myriad of non-sermon-related activities would impair the ability to learn from the content of a sermon. However, it turns out that it's not just using a smart phone *but the mere presence* of the technology is disruptive. That is, for example, just having one's phone in reach can limit what is learned.

This phenomenon was discovered in research conducted by Adrian Ward and his colleagues investigating consumer decision making. In one laboratory study, they assigned college students to one of three conditions: 1) students who had to leave their phones outside the lab (i.e., not accessible to them); 2) students who kept their phones with them, but in their pocket, backpack, purse, etc.; and 3) students who were allowed to keep their phones out and accessible to them. All students completed tasks related to learning and recall, including solving math problems, remembering a sequence of letters, and other measures of working memory capacity. The researcher found that the students without access to their phones performed the best on these tasks; students with their phones out and accessible to them fared worst. Of note was the finding students in Condition 2—merely having a cell phone in a nearby purse, bag, or pocket—also suffered a decrease in performance. According to the researchers:

> "Even when people are successful at maintaining sustained attention—as when avoiding the temptation to check their phones—the mere presence of these devices reduces available cognitive capacity. Moreover, these cognitive costs are highest for those highest in smartphone dependence. The more consumers depend on their smartphones, the more they seem to suffer from their presence—or, more optimistically, the more they may stand to benefit from their absence."[54]

What application can be made of these findings? I'm not sure. I do know that an admonition for congregants to leave their cellphones in the car, or to check them at the sanctuary door is unrealistic. I do, however, think that there may be ways to encourage listeners to disconnect from their phones during sermons in the interest of fostering greater ability to learn, recall, and apply more of what they hear.

CONCLUSIONS

This chapter provided several ways in which cognitive science can inform practical aspects of developing and delivering a sermon. We looked at principles related to density, piloting, parsimony, and visual effects in slide deck presentations. We saw how the incorporation of images, stories, examples and (sometimes) non-examples can help listeners grasp, retain, and use Biblical concepts in their lives. These principles should not be confused with rules. In each case, a speaker who is familiar with the audience—their backgrounds, needs, sensitivities, and prior learning—is in the best position to determine how these learning principles might be applied in any specific context.

---

54. Ward, Duke, Gneezy, and Bos, *Brain Drain*, 140.

CHAPTER 6

Testing 1, 2, 3

IN MANY CONGREGATIONS, THE conclusion of a church service includes what might be the most awkward moment of the entire time a pastor interacts with a congregation. Here is a description of what often occurs.

At the end of the service, a minister who has just delivered a sermon walks to the back of the church and greets the congregants as they leave. As they hug, shake hands, or just make eye contact, some departing church members might briefly comment on the sermon, saying something like "Great sermon, preacher!" Others may offer well wishes, "Have a good week, pastor." Still others might just politely say "Hello."

It's not clear what any of this means. There are typically few comments about the sermon. According to research reported by Lori Carrell, the vast majority of those who hear a sermon—78%–don't talk to preachers about their sermons.[1] None usually provide any specifics. Any comments certainly don't provide feedback that would be helpful to the pastor in terms of understanding *what* a listener thought was great about the sermon.

If indeed the sermon was "great," what made it so? Maybe that comment had nothing to do with the sermon at all but was just a social nicety like "Have a good week" or "Hello." Most importantly, such comments don't provide any information about what those in attendance actually *learned* from the sermon—or whether they learned anything at all. If I were standing there in the minister's place, the interaction that would trouble me the most would be the handshake without words. My anxiety would come from hearing in the back of my mind an admonition my mother oft repeated when I was growing up: "If you don't have something nice to say. . . "

---

1. Carrell, *The Great American Sermon Survey*.

THE IMPERATIVE FOR INFORMATION

After teaching in elementary school for five years, I decided that I should go back to school myself. In my doctoral program, I was immersed in learning about instructional design and strategies to improve my teaching. Four years of my graduate work involved teaching educational psychology—the study of how people learn.

Eventually, I focused my research and attention in the area of testing: measuring *how we know if people have learned*. I specialized in developing and evaluating methods for measuring their learning, and strategies for ensuring that the information we obtain about their learning is fair, accurate, and efficient. For our purposes, that focus has helped me answer what is arguably the most important question that could be asked following a sermon: "How do we know what our listeners have learned?"

Regrettably, that question is rarely asked about sermons.

According to Carrell, "It is extremely rare for a preacher to have a formal process for soliciting input or instigating dialogue before, during or after the sermon."[2] Of all the preachers surveyed in Carrell's study, only one used a formal feedback procedure; the most commonly used approach was to monitor listeners' facial expressions. In interviews conducted for that research, she found that preachers also rarely employ an interactive sermon approach that might elicit real-time feedback. Clinton Guthrie has emphasized the importance of getting feedback, writing that:

> "Preaching is simply too common and claims for its (celebrated or lamented) effectiveness too strident for [its effectiveness] not to deserve more attention from theorists and investigators of religion."[3]

ARE YOU SAYING TO GIVE TESTS IN CHURCH?

Yes.

With tongue in cheek, I'll provide two Scriptural references to support my response. For one, there is a clear direction in I Thessalonians:

---

2. Carrell, *The Great American Sermon Survey*, 123.
3. Guthrie, "Quantitative Empirical Studies of Preaching," 108.

"test everything"[4]

And, although I recognize that many—perhaps most—people don't like tests, God's promise in James is clear:

"God blesses those who patiently endure testing."[5]

Kidding aside, I'm not talking about testing in the way most people might think of it. Technically, the term *test* refers to any procedure for collecting a sample of a person's attitude, opinion, knowledge, or behavior obtained and interpreted in a uniform way as the information gained from others. That allows the information to be aggregated, analyzed, compared, and interpreted. According to this definition, informal questioning could qualify as a test, an opinion survey would be a test, and so on. So, to be clear, I'm *not* suggesting bubble sheets and No. 2 pencils be distributed following a sermon.

What I *am* suggesting is that if we are truly serious about finding out what sermon listeners have taken away from a sermon—if we want to know what they have learned—we must identify and incorporate testing into ecclesiastical practice in some way. The preachers surveyed by Carrell indicated the primary goal for their sermons. Those goals, and the percentages having each goal are reproduced in Table 6-1.

Table 6-1

Preachers' Self-Reported Primary Goals for their Sermons

Primary Goal	Percentage
to change hearers' beliefs, values, or actions	54%
to translate Biblical truth to today's culture	17%
to inspire	13%
to transmit information	11%

Apparently, however, homilists rarely get any information about the degree to which their goals are accomplished. Even in cases where they obtain *some* information, preachers typically have no way of judging the extent to which the information is accurate, whether the opinions are more

---

4. I Thessalonians 5:21a

5. James 1:12a

widely held or representative of other listeners, or the extent to which the information is idiosyncratic with respect to a single sermon versus generalizable across their sermons. Guthrie has made this point as well, advocating for more rigorous ways of obtaining information about the learning effects of sermons: "Since homileticians often give practical advice to preachers, it is desirable that they can back up their advice up with evidence of its effectiveness." Too often the evidence is [merely] anecdotal."[6] It is difficult to really make any specific conclusions about sermon content or delivery from even the warmest and most sincere comments, since often they are brief and general as in, "Great sermon, preacher."

TWO BENEFITS OF ASSESSMENT IN THE CONTEXT OF SERMONS

To avoid the association multiple-choice questions and No. 2 pencils, and because the term *test* carries a lot of baggage—e.g., grading, anxiety, bad memories from schooling, fear of evaluation, punitive uses, and so on—I'll switch to a term that evokes far fewer negative connotations: *assessment*. In the balance of this chapter, I'll use the term assessment to refer to procedures for information collection that results in accurate, dependable information and that permits the information to be confidently interpreted and, most importantly, used. Conducting assessment yields two benefits.

INFORMATION ABOUT THE PREACHING

A first benefit of engaging in assessment is that it provides information to the preacher about the sermon itself. The term used for this kind of information is *feedback*. The procedures used to obtain the feedback are called *formative assessment*. Perhaps no other topics in the learning sciences have received as much attention as formative assessment and feedback.

Formative Assessment

The concept of formative assessment has origins in the late 1960s and early 1970s related to paradigms for doing the work of evaluating curriculum, teaching and, more generally, any social program or organizational activity

---

6. Guthrie, "Quantitative Empirical Studies of Preaching," 100.

for which it was desired to know something about its effectiveness. Michael Scriven[7] and Benjamin Bloom and his colleagues[8] are credited with first using the terms *summative evaluation* and *formative evaluation* to refer to each of two different aims that a program evaluation might have.

In simple terms, Bloom referred to summative evaluation as a judgment about the program after the program or intervention was complete. Information would be gathered about the program and a judgment would be made regarding the value of the program. The judgment could take the form of *Continue/Discontinue Funding* for the program, the program was *Successful/Not Successful,* or similar conclusion that was, in a sense, final. That is, the program had run its course; there could not be any modifications introduced that might benefit those served by the program at that point.

By contrast, Bloom described formative evaluation as on-going. It comprised information gathering and use of that information during the course of the program that might suggest beneficial changes that could be implemented. Formative evaluation occurring before the conclusion of a program or intervention allows for course corrections to be made. What formative evaluation offers is not a final judgment, but information that could be used to build on program strengths, correct errors, address inadequacies, and improve the effectiveness of the program. It was not final, but formative. On a personal note, I have benefitted greatly from the candid comments on my teaching provided by the thousands of students over the years who completed instructional evaluation surveys in my courses. Those have included both formative, mid-course evaluations ("What can I do better this semester?") and summative, end-of-semester evaluations ("On a scale of 1-5, how would you rate the quality of teaching you received in this course?").

In the years since Scriven and Bloom introduced the concepts, abundant research has been conducted, particularly on formative evaluation—now referred to as *formative assessment*[9] to avoid the negative connotations of being "evaluated." Formative assessment is now conceptualized as a collaborative process in which one party—for example a preacher—and

---

7. Scriven, *The Methodology of Evaluation.*

8. Bloom, Hastings, and Madaus, *Handbook of Formative and Summative Evaluation of Student Learning.*

9. See, for example, Andrade and Cizek, *Handbook of Formative Assessment*; Cizek and Lim, "Formative Assessment."

other entity—for example, a colleague, a trusted confidant, a caring parishioner—engage in information gathering, debriefing, and planning with respect to whatever goals the preacher has for his or her sermons. Broadly speaking, the information to be communicated and considered is referred to as *feedback*.

Feedback

In their oft-referenced review of research on feedback John Hattie and Helen Timperley defined feedback as "information provided by an agent (e.g., teacher, peer, book, parent, self, experience) regarding aspects of one's performance or understanding" and they summarized research showing an unusually powerful effect of research on learning.[10] In a slightly less technical way, Grant Wiggins has defined feedback as "information about how we are doing in our efforts to reach a goal," and he provided three concrete examples of feedback:

> *Example 1* - A friend says, "You know, when you put it that way and speak in that softer tone of voice, it makes me feel better."
>
> *Example 2* - A reader comments on my short story, "The first few paragraphs kept my full attention. The scene painted was vivid and interesting. But then the dialogue became hard to follow; as a reader, I was confused about who was talking, and the sequence of actions was puzzling, so I became less engaged."
>
> *Example 3* - A baseball coach tells me, "Each time you swung and missed, you raised your head as you swung so you didn't really have your eye on the ball. On the one you hit hard, you kept your head down and saw the ball."[11]

It can be recognized that the kind of feedback implied by the definitions and discernable in the examples is *formative* feedback. That is, it is intended to be useful for making beneficial revisions. It is provided in the course of a conversation, while reading a short story, or during batting practice. There is time to make changes.

---

10. Hattie and Timperley, "The Power of Feedback," 81.
11. Wiggins, "Seven Keys to Effective Feedback," 10

A first principle to be noted about formative feedback is that it is information provided relevant to a goal that a person has. In Example 1, my friend and I share a mutual goal: better communication. In Example 2, I want to improve my writing. My goal in Example 3 is to become a better baseball player. Each of the three examples above illustrates different feedback relevant to a different goal. The three examples also subtly exemplify the characteristics that learning scientists have identified as the essential to effective feedback. Referring back to a finding from Carrell's survey on preaching shown in Table 6-1, the most frequently cited goal for developing and delivering sermons is "to change hearers' beliefs, values, or actions." If that is the goal for a sermon, what would formative feedback relevant to that goal look like?

Characteristics of Effective Feedback

It is perhaps first important to state two things that effective feedback is not. For one, it's not general or vague (a la, "Great sermon, preacher"). That comment may be nice to hear, but it lacks specifics, so it has no potential to affect how the preacher will prepare or deliver his or her next sermon. Second, it is not evaluative (as in "The way you always use examples from your family is getting pretty old."). Such a comment is somewhat specific but is likely discouraging to hear and can be taken as criticism of the person.

What makes for effective feedback? Many researchers have examined how feedback improves learning;[12] at least five characteristics of effective feedback are consistently identified. Table 6-2 lists the five characteristics and provides corresponding sermon-relevant examples.

---

12. For a comprehensive and accessible summary of this research, see Brookhart, *How to Give Effective Feedback*.

Table 6-2

Characteristics and Examples of Effective Feedback on Sermons

Effective feedback is . . .	*Example*
Goal-relevant	"That really helped me think about the 8th commandment in a different way when you gave that example of taking home office supplies from work."
Specific	"Can you speak more often from the center of the room? That seemed to give us all a better sense of 'connection' when it feels like you are right here with us instead of up in the pulpit."
Timely	"Oh, wait! I've never even heard of *imprecatory* prayer. What are some times in the Bible when God answered that kind of a prayer?"
Constructive	"I think if you gave us a bit more time to take notes or provided an outline of the key points of the sermon, that would be really helpful."
Actionable	"There are quite a few of us who have difficulty hearing. Would it be possible to reserve a row or two up front for us, or maybe could you just turn up the volume a bit?"

First, effective feedback is goal relevant. In the context of preaching, that means it comprises information bearing on what the homilist was trying to accomplish in a sermon. Feedback on a preacher's nice haircut, scarf, posture, or smile would be effective if the homilist's goal was sartorial, demeanor, or hygienic impression; it would have no effect on the goal of helping a congregation to understand the principle of tithing.

Second, effective feedback is specific. Specific feedback communicates clearly what was helpful (or harmful) about some aspect of a sermon. "Giving another example or two of that would really help clarify for me what you mean." "It feels like you have favorites or don't really value what the rest of us do when you always use Deacon Ralph as your example for someone who works tirelessly for our ministries. Just spreading the accolades around a bit would be nice."

Third, effective feedback is timely. That is, it is provided in close temporal proximity to the actions it has the potential to effect. Specific observations provided in an email the day after a sermon will be more effective than the same specific observations held onto and voiced later at the quarterly church council meeting.

Fourth, effective feedback is constructive. The heart of the person giving the feedback matters. Whatever input is given should reflect genuine concern and goodwill. It should be presented in such a way that the recipient perceives the giver as earnestly and unequivocally "on my side." Not all feedback must be positive. Constructive feedback that provides input about what *not* to do can be effective, but it should not be framed or received as critical, overly negative, or as a personal attack.

Fifth, effective feedback is actionable. The recipient must be able to *do* something with the information to aid him or her in accomplishing their goal. Kindheartedly letting a speaker know that his or her sermons are hard to hear and offering the specific suggestions of just turning up the volume a bit or designating seating for the hard of hearing is actionable. Telling a speaker that his or her deep southern accent is distracting is not.

The Role of Feedback

I will now make the obvious connection between the concepts of formative assessment and feedback that is relevant to developing and delivering sermons. Information gained about one's sermons (i.e., feedback) can be used to make changes along the way (i.e., formatively) so that greater learning from them occurs and they have greater impact on the lives of listeners. I'll assume that all preachers—certainly all readers of this book—actually *want* this kind of information. To be specific, those of us with the calling and heart of teachers aren't asking listeners to "Please punch me in the gut" or "Tell me everything I'm doing wrong." What we want to get is information about how we can spiritually enrich our listeners, how we can help them learn and apply more of what we are preaching about, what barriers to their learning we can help tear down, what we can do so that the spoken word might have a greater impact in their lives.

At the outset, I should qualify what I mean by "along the way." I am *not* suggesting that sermons should be interrupted with questions, pleas for additional examples, requests for clarifications, rebuttals, and so on. There may be a time or place when these kinds of "along the way" sources of information might be appropriate, but I'll proceed as if the time and place are not in the middle of a Sabbath day service. I'm conceptualizing "along the way" as over the course of a sermon series, over the weeks, months, or even years that a preacher is connected with a congregation. A first sermon given to a congregation might start that connection, but it doesn't end when that sermon concludes. It is ongoing until the last sermon to them is preached. That is, information obtained as feedback after any particular sermon has the potential to be used formatively to make in-process adjustments for all following sermons.

Feedback and Power

Now the really challenging part: How might such formative feedback be gained? Shortly, we'll examine four approaches to gathering information about one's preaching, but I'll begin with background on two factors that should be considered prior to developing or implementing any plan for soliciting formative feedback. Both have to do with power differentials. The first factor has to do with power differentials between individuals.

By *power differentials*, I mean the differences in status or authority that exist between persons in differing positions. Let's consider an ostensibly "easy" way that a preacher might solicit feedback about a recent sermon from members of a congregation. The preacher might simply converse with an individual member informally or set up a weeknight meeting with a small group and ask: "What were your impressions of the sermon last Sunday? Please be as honest as possible; I'm genuinely interested in what is working and what I can do better."

As genuine and well-meaning as the pastor might be, there is a barrier to honest communication that exists because of the power differential at play. Many church members may feel reluctant to express an honest opinion or give negative feedback to someone they consider to be their spiritual shepherd. Even if unfounded, their subconscious or conscious thoughts might be:

> "Who am I to say something bad about the sermon. Pastor knows so much more about that topic than I do."
>
> "If I say something that hurts his feelings or is negative, I wonder if I'll still be considered for the open slot on the Deacon Board."
>
> "I'm just a teenager. I doubt my comments will be taken seriously. He'll probably just think I'm being a smart ass."

> *"My mother is in the hospital, and I was just going to ask Pastor to visit her. This would not be a good time for me to give any honest reactions to his sermon."*
>
> *"In our church, it just wouldn't be right for a woman to offer any critique of our male pastor."*
>
> *"I've only been attending this church for the last few weeks. I'd better just keep quiet and be respectful of the Pastor."*

In each of these hypothetical musings, the person is concerned about the potential, however small or unwarranted, of some negative consequence for them of providing honest input. The caution here is that powerful differentials are omnipresent, and they invariably operate to a greater or lesser extent between individuals of different perceived status based on position, age, sex, ethnicity, social class, and other characteristics. For example, real or perceived power differentials may have underlied Carrell's finding that many women hearers were reluctant to speak to their male preachers. Because they are always at play, any information acquired in an interaction in which power differentials exist must be considered as potentially inaccurate to some (unknown) degree. Fortunately, as we will see, there are workarounds to the presence of power differentials.

The second factor has to do with perspectives regarding appropriate roles that are embedded in cultural norms, and it relates to an earlier idea presented in this book—the notion that preaching must be sensitive to listener characteristics. Here's a specific example: I presented some of the information on the idea of "testing" in church to the PhD in Preaching cohort at Truett Theological Seminary in Waco, Texas. After the seminar, I got an email from one of the students, Timothy Rhee, who wanted to discuss the idea at greater length.[13] Tim saw the value of testing—that is, getting formative information about one's preaching—but challenged me to consider whether endorsing such information gathering as a universally good practice was appropriate.

We talked about his experience attending and pastoring primarily Asian/North American congregations in Illinois. He also introduced me to Geert Hofstede's cultural dimensions theory.[14] Hofstede postulated a framework comprising five aspects that characterize cultural differences

---

13. I am grateful for that conversation and the insights provided by Timothy Y. Rhee, PhD, for all of what follows on this topic. Any misunderstandings or misrepresentations on my part are solely my responsibility.

14. See Hofstede, "Culture and Organizations," and *Culture's Consequences*.

across countries. His Power-Distance Index is relevant to the potential for a preacher to acquire accurate feedback on a sermon. The Power Distance Index is a measure of the degree to which members of a group (Hofstede studied organizational and institutional power) accept and expect that power is distributed equally. He observed that, although there is a certain degree of inequality in all societies, there is relatively more equality in some societies than in others. In cultures with a high Power Distance Index, individuals, often tacitly, accept power hierarchies without the need for justification. Other cultures where low Power Distance is the norm are characterized by greater equality of distribution of power among individuals and expectations that relations are more consultative, democratic, or egalitarian.

Tim invoked this theoretical perspective in describing how soliciting information about a sermon might be possible in a typical suburban evangelical Protestant church in the U.S. where the congregation was predominately white, native born, and English speaking. Among that group—*as a cultural group*—a lower Power Index would exist and cultural norms would not militate against individual members offering honest critique of someone in a position of status (i.e., a pastor) within the organization (i.e., church). He described the much different situation that might exist in a church such as he pastored, where a higher Power Index existed. In that congregation, comprising primarily North American Asians, congregants operated under a cultural norm of accepted power hierarchies. Tim averred that the accepted cultural norms would likely not support any information gathering process that could be perceived as evaluative or disrespectful toward a person in power (e.g. the pastor) regardless of how well intentioned. To some degree, the same situation could be experienced in Latino, African American, or multicultural preaching contexts. In any context, it seems wise to consider the power differentials and cultural norms that may affect the nature and prospect of obtaining sermon feedback.

Potential Sources of Information

Despite the existence of power differentials, a variety of possibilities exist for the preacher interested in gaining accurate, helpful information about his or her sermons. Some mechanisms are more informal and unstructured than others, but nonetheless provide the speaker with some information about how a sermon is being received. In some faith traditions, giving feedback is an expectation or cultural norm. It is not solicited; it just breaks forth. For example, in many African American and other churches it is not uncommon for a congregant to proclaim:

"*Preach it, brother!*" (to indicate agreement with a point made in a sermon)

"*Come on, Pastor: Make it plain!*" (to indicate that a point is not clear)

"*We see the cookies on the shelf, but bring it down!*" (to request great accessibility).

Other mechanisms are more formal, more structured, and more amenable to thoughtful reflection on the meaning of the feedback they provoke.

Dialogic Preaching

A formalization of the kinds of preacher-listener/learner interactions illustrated above is a preaching style sometimes referred to as *dialogic preaching*. This orientation derived from the work of Mikhail Bakhtin, a Russian philosopher and literary critic whose written work was produced between approximately 1919 and 1961. Among that work, Bakhtin's dialogic theory influenced the so-called New Homiletics paradigm influential in western countries from the late 1960s through the 1990s.[15] The dialogic approach conceptualizes sermons not as monologues, but as two-way interactions, conversations, dialogues among entities.[16]

A contemporary interpretation of dialogic preaching is described by an advocate of the approach, Dan White, Jr. who characterizes the preaching of Jesus, Peter, and Paul as dialogic. That is, their teachings consisted largely of interactions with listeners where questions were posed, answered, and conversations occurred.[17] Another contemporary explication of dialogic preaching is given by Floyd Bresee, who described the style of consisting of four elements; the third of which seems to best characterize the dialogic approach:

> "Invite input. Announce your Scriptural passage and invite members to read it and then to come to a meeting at which they will share ideas, illustrations, and real-life applications of that passage.

---

15. See Lorensen, *Dialogic Preaching*.

16. Based on her survey results, Carrell found this approach to be extremely rare in practice, with most preachers saying they would "rarely" or "never" ask a question for which they wanted a verbal answer from a sermon listener.

17. White, *The Act of Dialogical Preaching*.

Use rhetorical questions in your sermons. Try a dialogue sermon in which you share the pulpit with another speaker. One may take the part of the listener and ask questions the congregation might want asked."[18]

Self-Recording

Perhaps the most straightforward method for getting potentially helpful feedback on a sermon is an adaptation of the strategy I used, described in Chapter 1, when I first began teaching in elementary school. The strategy consisted of putting a high-capacity tape into a portable cassette recorder, placing the recorder in an unobtrusive location, and pressing the "Record" button. My attempt wasn't high-tech, but effective.

The same self-recording and reflection approach would be much more easily facilitated by modern technology. In fact, it is likely that the information is already collected and available for review. Many sermons are now live-streamed, recorded, and archived, and include not only the limited information gained by the audio-only approach that I had used, but also video so that mannerisms, gestures, eye-contact, audience reactions, and other non-verbal information is available. As I found, the low-threat activity of just listening to myself giving a presentation permitted the opportunity to self-identify habits of which I had previously been unaware. Video recording offers even greater potential for thoughtful and honest self-assessment.

A variation of this approach that can be of greater benefit is review of the recorded sermon with a trusted friend, colleague, or coach. I'll elaborate in much greater detail on how this might be done in Chapter 7.

Surveys

Another mechanism for gathering formative information about a sermon is by actively soliciting feedback via a survey approach. Such a survey could take various forms, but the first important characteristic of this methodology is that it is anonymous or at least offers the possibility of anonymity. To avoid the possible effect of the power differentials just described, solicitations of feedback can be accomplished such that individual listeners' concerns about potential ramifications of honest input are assuaged.

18. Bresee, "How to Be a Dialogical Preacher," 23.

Testing 1, 2, 3

In many congregations today, some variation of a feedback instrument already exists. In several different churches I've attended, there are small cards at the end of each pew, in seat backs, or in other locations among the congregation. The cards are referred to by various names depending on the specific locale. "Connect Card," "View from the Pew," or similar names are used as titles for the cards where listeners on any given occasion can check boxes such as those shown in Figure 6-1.

Figure 6-1

```
☐ Please have a pastor contact me.
☐ I have made a decision to accept Jesus.
☐ I would like prayer for _____.
☐ I would like more information about the
   _____ ministry.
☐ I would like to volunteer for _____.
☐ Other (describe): _____
   _____
```

Example of Congregation Response Card

Congregants are asked, typically near the end of a service, to complete the items on the card, with the understanding, often explicitly stated, that responding to items on the card is voluntary and optional. The cards are then collected in an anonymous way, often by respondents dropping them in a collection basket passed down the rows of a meeting space, or deposited in a box for tithes/offerings/feedback cards at specified locations in a sanctuary.

Technology also facilitates electronic versions of this feedback mechanism. For example, the same check-box items could appear as an anonymous feedback form on a church's website or via a phone-based app.[19]

---

19. Web-based or cell phone-based app collection of feedback might be viewed as potentially less anonymous by potential respondents. Although it is true that a respondent's identity (IP address, cell phone number) could be discerned if a web- or phone-based approach is used, any explicit assurance of anonymity should obviously be respected. Further, even if an explicit assurance is not made, most respondents would likely assume such.

Regardless of mode of collection, the check box item format has great appeal inherent in its efficiency. It takes little time for respondents to indicate their responses; this characteristic is known to promote a greater response rate. The principle is universal: the less anonymous and longer it takes to complete a survey or questionnaire, the fewer people are likely to complete it and the less representative the resulting information is likely to be.

In many educational contexts, teachers have used a variation of this approach to get parallel information about a lecture. For example, in my own courses, I will occasionally ask students as a class is ending to simply make a mark on a survey placed near the exit to the lecture hall. The survey and hypothetical responses might look something like that shown in Figure 6-2. Such an approach has given me valuable information about how clear the information was perceived to be, students' views of how helpful an in-class activity was, and other aspects of what I had planned and presented. I was able to use that information to consider beginning the next class meeting with a review and additional explanation of the concepts covered in the previous week, to consider revising, deleting, adding to the examples I had thought might be beneficial, and so on.

Figure 6-2

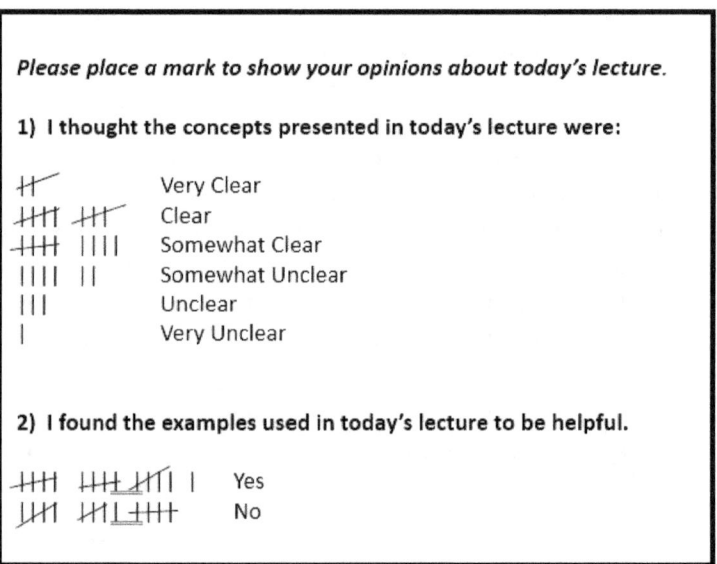

Gathering Feedback on a Presentation

Extending that approach to gathering formative information about a sermon, it would be a simple matter to implement a new feedback collection initiative using a response card or web- or app-based survey. Or, if an existing information collection mechanism exists such as a paper Connect Card or app-based questionnaire, it would be even easier to build on it by supplementing the existing items with additional items specifically related to the sermon. Referring back to Figure 6-2, we can imagine simply replacing the word "lecture" with "sermon" for a beginning illustration of what such items might look like. In actual practice, the exact wording of any items would depend on what the preacher wanted to know about his or her sermon. Further, any items would need to be developed with greater care than might be inferred from the two hypothetical items shown in Figure 6-2. The actual wording of any items and accompanying response options would need to be developed and reviewed for readability, clarity, focus, and for what potential respondents interpreted each item as asking.

One additional note: The items shown in Figure 6-2 are classified as "closed-end" or "select-response" type items. There is a large menu of options for select-response items, including the familiar multiple-choice format with pre-determined response options, a simple *Yes/No, True/False, or Agree/Disagree* format, as well as the equally familiar Likert-style format with response choices such as *Strongly Disagree, Disagree, Neutral, Agree,* and *Strongly Agree*. Some advantages of these formats are their familiarity to respondents, and their efficiency. Research has demonstrated that items using these formats are more likely to actually be responded to because they don't require much effort to do so.

By contrast, items that are "open ended" or "constructed response" are less efficient because respondents must craft and enter their own responses. An example of some constructed-response format items for gaining feedback on the sermon content and presentation is provided in Figure 6-3.[20] Open-ended items take more time to respond to and, as a consequence, response rates are typically lower for items using these formats. The limitations notwithstanding, there is also an obvious benefit to using constructed-response items for getting information about the preaching. A greater amount of feedback is obtained; respondents are not constrained by a slate of predetermined responses provided for them to consider; there is greater opportunity for respondents to organize and express their own

---

20. The examples shown in Figures 6-2 and 6-3 as well as additional questions that might be used are available for free download in the Resources section of www.SermonScience.com

comments; and more elaborated responses are likely, including responses that may contain valuable information, but which are not expressly related to a question that was asked.[21]

Figure 6-3

Please write/enter your responses to the following questions in the space provided.

1) What would you say was the most unclear point about the sermon today?

_____
_____
_____

2) If there was an example given in today's sermon that you found particularly helpful, what was it?

_____
_____
_____

3) In what way, if any, would you say that the sermon today could have better addressed some questions you have about [sermon topic]?

_____
_____
_____

4) Was there anything about today's sermon (e.g., volume, ability to see what was projected, length) that you would say could be improved?

_____
_____
_____

Example of Feeback Collection Using Open-Ended Format Questions

21. Abundant research and guidelines exist regarding survey approaches for gathering formative feedback, including information on how to create them, methods for delivering them, strategies for increasing response rates and representativeness, and methods for investigating the reliability and validity of the information gained. Among them are Colton and Covert, *Designing and Constructing Instruments for Social Research and Evaluation*, and Dillman, Smyth, and Christian, *Internet, Phone, Mail, and Mixed-mode Surveys*.

Preaching Circles

Finally, the technique of *preaching circles* has received some attention as a mechanism for obtaining formative sermon feedback. Implementations of the technique vary from a more basic configuration where a preacher simply presents a proposed sermon in advance to a (usually small), select group of trusted advisors, representative church members, or perhaps simply interested and willing congregants. The presentation may be more dialogic, with questions, interruptions, and discussions along the way, or a debriefing may occur at the conclusion of the presentation. If the former, it is likely that semi-formal "rules" to guide the interactions should be developed and affirmed by those participating. If the latter, it is most productive and informative if the debriefing consists of structured set of questions, similar to those that might be used in a preaching survey.

One variation of a preaching circle has been described in the context of Catholic lay leadership. The Catholic Women's Preaching Circle (CWPC) is characterized as:

> "an initiative to support Catholic women desiring to grow in the skill of breaking open the Word of God. This peer-led space offers the opportunity to create and deliver a [sermon] and practice giving and receiving feedback. Each CWPC cohort is made up of six or seven participants, and one or two conveners."[22]

A second variation is described by Gerald Procee in which he reflects on his personal experience with the approach:

> "I have the privilege to belong to a preaching circle under the chairmanship of Rev. P. den Butter. We come together with a group of seven ministers who serve actively in the ministry and three emeritus ministers. The former minister of Dundas, Rev. K. Hoefnagel also belongs to this preaching circle. The chair assigns a text by rotation to each member and appoints three men to offer critique.
>
> The sermon is written out in full and submitted a week before each meeting, which is held about five times per year. The three ministers designated to offer critique are first given the opportunity to voice their comments, and subsequently every member has an opportunity to voice his opinion. The final critique is allotted to the chairman. What makes these gatherings so valuable is that

---

22. See "About Catholic Women's Preaching Circle," https://sites.google.com/view/catholicwomenspreachingcircle/home/about

the chair offers not only critique but supplies also a sermon outline of how he would handle such a text. The results of such preaching sessions may then be utilized for each person's preaching."[23]

Procee's description is similar to what is called "student teaching" in K-12 schooling contexts. In that context an aspiring teacher plans and presents a lesson in a real, classroom context. The lesson is observed by other teachers-in-training and a master teacher who provide feedback and formative suggestions afterward.

Overall, it appears that the technique of preaching circles for obtaining formative information about sermon development and delivery is more recognized in principle than in practice. Specific definitions and descriptions are few and there appear to be limited examples of it in use. There exists abundant research and guidelines on survey approaches for gathering formative feedback, including information on how to create them, methods for delivering them, strategies for increasing response rates and representativeness, and methods for investigating the reliability and validity of the information gained. By contrast however, little if any research exists on best practices for creating dialogic sermons or preaching circles;[24] evidence is not available on the effectiveness of those approaches, in isolation or compared to other strategies, for enhancing listeners' understanding, recall, or application of sermon content.

Summary

The focus of this section has been on gathering information about the preaching. The purpose for collecting this information is to aid in self-development, to refine one's preaching approach, to discover aspects that can be considered for making adjustments to style, habits, delivery, organization, and other aspects of a sermon related to the one giving the sermon.

A preacher wishing to get formative feedback about his or her sermons has several tools that can aid in doing so. The rapid pace of technological development promises that new tools will also soon be available. One prominent development is Artificial Intelligence (AI), a technology that portends many applications to modern life that are at present not even imagined. The practice of preaching will certainly be affected. For example,

23. Prosee, "Preaching Circles."
24. For example, Carrell's survey found that preachers rarely engage in dialogue sermons with their congregations.

AI has now been applied to automating translations of sermon content into blog posts, devotionals, social media posts, and communications with congregants.[25] Almost certainly, AI and other emerging technologies will soon be available to assist in creating, summarizing, and interpreting information about the content of actual preaching events. Even existing technologies for presenting sermon content and communicating with listeners, church members, and those we seek to evangelize will likely evolve and, in just the next decade, be unrecognizable from applications used for those purposes today.

The impact of those developments on how learning occurs is unknown. For now, however, there are learning principles that apply to gathering feedback about sermons that influence the extent to which listeners' input can have the intended positive effects. Feedback should be sought in a timely way; specific information should be solicited; the feedback should be constructive, related to the goals for the sermon, and actionable. Even modest attempts will be rewarded. Regardless of the method selected, the initiative of seeking formative feedback will have a downstream impact on sermon listeners, helping them to better grasp, retain, and use the intended concepts.

INFORMATION ABOUT THE LEARNING

In a previous section, I described an applied subfield of educational psychology called *program evaluation*, where a "program" is conceptualized as essentially any intervention, plan, organizational activity, or policy. Program evaluators' primary concern is the development and deployment of methods for understanding questions such as whether a program is working, how it might be improved, or whether the costs of a program are justified by its benefits. The work of creating and delivering a sermon would, by this definition, qualify as a "program."

Program evaluators sometimes describe the three main aims of their work as answering the following questions that reflect the analogy of planning a trip: 1) "Where do I want to go?" 2) "How do I get there?" and 3) "How do I know when I'm getting closer?"

Applied to the context of creating and delivering sermons, the parallels to the three main concerns of preaching are clear:

---

25. See https://pulpitai.com/

1) *What do I want my listeners to take away from my sermon?* (That is, what do I have as the goals for my sermon in terms of what I'd like listeners to learn from my sermon and be able to apply to their lives?)

2) *What can I do to help them learn what I have in mind?* (That is, how can I create and develop a sermon that is focused on those goals?)

3) *How will I know if I was successful?* (That is, what information can I get that will help me understand if my listeners have learned what I had intended?)

The first question is beyond the scope or purpose of this book. What the topic of a sermon will be is determined by the preacher; the learning sciences have nothing to say about that. Preceding chapters of this book have provided some principles from the field of instructional design that bear on the second question—helping listeners learn—but there are many other elements on that question which are not addressed in this book (e.g., preaching styles, speaking techniques, denominational traditions) that come into play. The third question, arguably the most important one, is the focus of this section. It is the question that is rarely asked—and even less often satisfactorily answered—regarding a sermon: *How do I know what my listeners learned from my sermon?*

Testing Reprised

Earlier in this chapter, I joked about giving tests in church. As the reader knows, I invoked the term *test* to refer to any systematic approach to information gathering. We then saw how such information gathering—formative assessment—could be helpful to a preacher interested in getting feedback for improving his or her sermons. The same logic applies to gathering information for the purpose of understanding what listeners actually took away from a sermon; that is, what they *learned*. In nearly every other context where we are interested in measuring learning, we give a test. So again, yes, tests should be given in ecclesiastical contexts if we want to answer the most important question of all following delivery of a sermon.

I'll tread cautiously here because *I get it*. The topic of testing likely brings to mind traumatic school-related experiences: the stress of taking the SAT, the deflation of getting a low grade on an assignment; the standardized test that doesn't allow you to explain your answer or the essay test that doesn't allow guessing from the A, B, C, or D choices but demands that you provide an explanation. We all suffer from some degree of testing anxiety.[26] Nonetheless, tests are common in all learning and the broad definition of "test" includes many variations that induce little or no anxiety compared to a graduate school entrance examination, driver's license test, or medical board exam.

We all know about tests, but what is not as widely known is that they not only measure learning, they also *cause* learning. By giving a test, one can not only get answers to the question of what listeners have learned, but the very act of giving a test has been shown to increase how much is learned. This cognitive principle, called not-so-creatively "the testing effect," is now well established. Few findings from the learning sciences make the front section of the *New York Times*, but this one did.[27]

Figure 6-4

> # The New York Times
> ## To Really Learn, Quit Studying and Take a Test
> By Pam Belluck
> Jan. 20, 2011
>
> Taking a test is not just a passive mechanism for assessing how much people know, according to new research. It actually helps people learn, and it works better than a number of other studying techniques.

The Learning Effect of Testing

The research underlying the testing effect is rather technical, dense, and complicated. However, an accurate summary would be this: People learn more when they know they will face a test assessing their learning after some instruction they will receive. The basis for the testing effect began with research in the mid-2000s.[28] Taking a test was shown to produce

---

26. For more information on the causes of and ways to address test anxiety, see Cizek and Burg, *Addressing Test Anxiety in a High-Stakes Environment*.
27. Belluck, "To Really Learn, Quit Studying and Take a Test," A14.
28. Roediger and Karpicke, "Test-Enhanced Learning."

greater learning than reviewing the material, study groups, cramming, additional reading on the topic, concept mapping, and other forms of practice.[29] The effect has been confirmed by other researchers as not only applying to simple recall of information, but also to learning complex concepts.[30]

The succinct translation for preaching: a congregation will grasp and retain more of a sermon's main ideas if they expect some kind of quiz about the sermon afterward.

How the Testing Effect Works

Again, let's reset. Findings about the testing effect from the learning sciences do *not* mean that a formal test should be developed, that congregants should be told there will be a test after the sermon, and that such a test should be administered (let alone graded and reported!). The nuanced interpretation of research on the testing effect in the context of preaching comprises two elements. First, it helps a congregation to learn more from a sermon if, before the sermon, they are told that they will be able to respond to what they have heard. Second, it is beneficial if, afterward, there is an opportunity to do so.

What would these two characteristics look like in practice? The first element is easily accomplished merely by stating it. Here's an example:

> *"At the conclusion of today's sermon, there will be an opportunity for everyone who wishes to do so, to reflect on some of what we will be hearing related to God's ideas for use of our money, to the topic of tithing, and His directions for helping the poor."*

Wording such as this could be included as a sermon preamble, in the introduction or, if the practice occurs regularly, it may not even need to be spoken if it is tacitly expected as part of an implemented tradition of information gathering.

How the testing effect operates is also known. It's *not* primarily due to the actual taking of a test. Rather, telling someone that they will be taking a test on X and Y at the conclusion of a lesson creates a cognitive frame for what is to come and imbues X and Y with an increased salience that it wouldn't have otherwise. Cognitively, the announcement subtly defines, *a*

---

29. McDaniel, Anderson, Derbish, and Morisett, "Testing the Testing Effect in the Classroom."

30. Karpicke and Aue, "The Testing Effect Is Alive and Well with Complex Materials."

priori, what should be attended to in the sermon. Alternatively, using the language of the program evaluator cited earlier, listeners have a preliminary answer to the first question in planning the trip: they now have a clearer idea of where we are going. Having that notion makes it more likely that they will get to the intended destination.

What Testing Might Look Like

Of course, it would be inappropriate to tell sermon listeners that there will be quiz at the conclusion of a sermon and not provide that opportunity. What might that opportunity look like? There are a variety of possibilities, many of which are similar to the approaches covered earlier in this chapter related to the formative, self-assessment information speakers might gather about their preaching. We'll now look at three potential strategies for getting exit information on learning.

EXIT TICKETS. Informal approaches to gathering information about what has been learned have been common in traditional teaching/schooling contexts for decades. For example, teachers have used what are referred to as "exit tickets" to informally gauge student learning at the end of a lesson. In elementary school classrooms, a teacher might require students to respond to a question in order to be dismissed for lunch, recess, or at the end of the day. Answering the question—whether correctly or incorrectly is largely irrelevant in terms of the individual students—provides the teacher with information about what was learned. . . or not. Examples of exit ticket prompts would be:

- What was one thing you learned today about our solar system?
- What stuck with you from our class today on adverbs?
- How confident are you that you can multiply fractions?
- If you had to tell a friend who missed class today about what the main thing we learned was, what would it be?
- Who is best known for first suggesting that the earth isn't flat?

Exit ticket prompts do not necessarily require written responses and need not be limited to knowledge gained from a lesson. For example, students might be asked to report on their feelings about something they learned (see Figure 6-5).

Figure 6-5

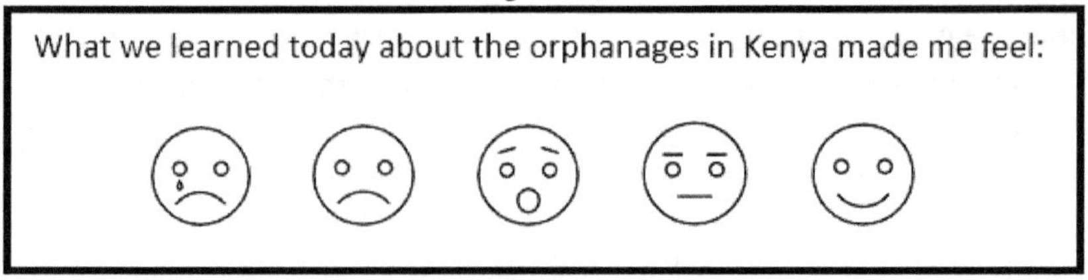

What we learned today about the orphanages in Kenya made me feel:

Example of "Exit Ticket"

Responses to an exit prompt can also be made orally, in writing, or using a common school technology involving clickers (see Figure 6-6). A clicker is a small device that students can use to indicate responses to exit (or other) questions; their responses are automatically collected and summarized for the teacher. Clicker use is not limited to elementary school classrooms; they are routinely used in large lectures at the secondary and college levels as well.

Figure 6-6

iClicker 2
READY
DELETE
SEND
A
B
C
D
E

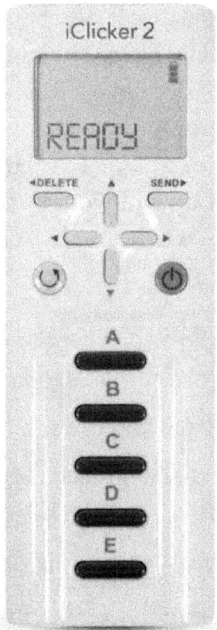

Using Technology to Gather Feedback

TESTING 1, 2, 3

Let's now apply these ideas to investigating what listeners learn from a sermon. Obviously, requiring congregants to answer questions to get permission to leave a church service would be inappropriate. The cost to purchase sufficient clickers for a large congregation would likely be prohibitive. In many traditions, the incorporation of such technology would not be acceptable. Nonetheless, the concepts and learning purposes behind exit tickets and clickers are readily adaptable to the contexts of sermons. In some cases, it may be of interest to understand congregants' affective responses to a sermon, using an age-appropriate parallel to the item shown in Figure 6-5. Ordinarily, however, it would be of greatest interest to gain insights into what listeners learned from sermon, what they found valuable, useful, or relevant to their lives. It would be desirable to understand the aspects about which there may have been some confusion, for which additional clarifications or examples would be helpful, or regarding how the content of a sermon one day related to the content of a sermon given last week or how it will relate to what will be presented in coming weeks. Questions such as those shown in Figure 6-7 might be asked.[31]

As was noted earlier in this chapter, in many churches today a paper response form, sermon notes page, or "Connect Card" is provided for those in attendance. Those existing avenues for information gathering could be supplemented with questions to gauge what was learned. Congregants wishing to provide feedback on what they learned can respond to and deposit in a designated location their responses to a sermon question inserted in the church bulletin, a tear-off portion of a sermon notes handout, or a separate question card relevant to a specific sermon.

In some contemporary congregations, the leadership and congregation members may feel comfortable with direct use of technology for viewing and responding to sermon questions, not only at the conclusion of a sermon, but even during a service. Freely downloadable cell phone-based apps such as Poll Everywhere[32] enable listeners to use their mobile devices to respond to selected-response format questions. Questions can be projected or viewed on cell phones; responses can be aggregated for later review, or results can be instantly summarized, graphically displayed, and projected in real time for presentation during a sermon.

---

31. The example shown in the figure as well as additional questions that might be used are available for free download in the Resources section of www.SermonScience.com

32. See https://www.polleverywhere.com/

Figure 6-7

> *Please write your responses to the following questions, using as little or as much of the space provided as you wish. All questions are optional.*
>
> 1) What would you say was the most unclear point about the sermon today?
> _____
> _____
> _____
>
> 2) What would you say are one or two key takeaways from today's sermon?
> _____
> _____
> _____
>
> 3) In what way, if any, would you say that the sermon today could have better addressed some questions you have about [sermon topic]?
> _____
> _____
> _____
>
> 4) In what practical ways do you think you will be use what you learned from today's sermon?
> _____
> _____

Example Questions for Gauging Sermon Learning

FOCUS GROUPS. Focus groups represent a longstanding approach to understanding people's knowledge, opinions, and attitudes. As the name implies, focus groups comprise a (usually) small group of participants who are assembled for the purpose of addressing one or more specific, focused questions that are of interest to a preacher, a synagogue education committee, Christian adult ministry coordinator, or other congregation leaders. They provide an opportunity for the initiators of the focus group to interact with a small number of selected participants who react to questions about a topic. Although focus groups begin with formal ideas about the questions to be asked, the format allows for participants to be probed for elaborations regarding their responses; participants can also interact, debate, and discuss the topic within the group so that, for example, a fuller, in-depth understanding of what was learned from a sermon, participants' reactions to a sermon, or what participants perceive to be their needs can be obtained.

Additional details on designing and conducting a focus group are beyond the scope of this chapter. Entire volumes have been devoted to procedures for recruiting participants for focus groups, for identifying optimal ways to structure the groups, for developing appropriate questions and probes for focus groups, for actually conducting a focus group meeting, and for synthesizing what can be learned from participants comments.[33] Following such procedures would be necessary in high-stakes contexts, for example when an investor is considering putting millions of dollars into a technology startup company. A focus group might be essential to gauge market interest in the product, user acceptance, or other potential applications of the technology. In the context of understanding what listeners have learned from a sermon, equally rigorous procedures are likely unnecessary. In their stead, a list of questions about what listeners took away from a sermon (similar, perhaps, to those shown in Figure 6-7) might be developed by the preacher and discussed in a small informal, non-evaluative weeknight gathering over coffee.

SURVEYS. A third option for information gathering for understanding what listeners have learned from a sermon parallels the survey approach described previously in this chapter for obtaining information for formative assessment. In this case, the target is not information regarding how the preacher might improve; the survey instrumentation would be developed to focus on finding out what listeners have learned. Accordingly, this section won't repeat everything presented earlier, except to be clear about the specific procedures that might be used.

Technically, although a formal survey might be used, I suspect that it would not (and maybe should not) be the norm. A traditional, paper version of a survey or an electronic version delivered by email or other method might be useful for a large-scale, congregation-wide data collection on

---

33. Detailed information on designing and conducting focus groups can be found in Krueger and Casey, *Focus Groups*, and Smithson, "Focus Groups."

questions such as approval for expenditure on a building project, support for starting a school associated with a local church, extending a call to a new head pastor, or merging with another local congregation. However, for "mini-inquiries" into what attendees learned from a sermon or sermon series, much smaller scale and more informal efforts are better aligned to that purpose. Thus, as described previously, pew-based comment cards, bulletin inserts, focus groups, "Coffee with the Pastor" night or—in some contexts—even a show of hands during or following a sermon would be more appropriate.

CONCLUSIONS

Three findings from the science of learning related to testing are clear:

1) Done with care, assessment can be a powerful tool for gathering information to improve preaching (that is, the formative orientation of assessment). Achieving this requires not only attention to potential methods that will result in the collection of dependable information, but also a measure of humility and openness on the part of the preacher to be willing to entertain and act on the information yielded.

2) Approached with equal care and respect for the norms and traditions of a congregation, assessment can be a powerful tool for gathering information to understand what listeners to a sermon have learned, what may have been misunderstood, and aid in planning a subsequent sermon or discussion session.

3) The benefit of assessment lies not only in a formative use for the preacher and its information about learning for the congregation, but the act of assessment itself also has the potential to increase learning.

In the first portion of this chapter covering the ways in which a preacher could obtain formative information to adjust his or her creation and delivery of sermons, four strategies were described: dialogic preaching, self-recording, surveys, and preaching circles. Based on my experience, a fifth option should be added to that list. That option is one that I have implemented in several contexts, but to my knowledge has not received the same attention in the literature on preaching as the others. I am commending this strategy—which I refer to as the "Critical Friend" approach as an ideal place to start for a preacher interested in improvement. Because the approach involves a number of essential elements to be described, I judged that it merited a chapter all of its own—Chapter 7—which follows both immediately and logically from the emphasis in this chapter on ways to obtain information about preaching and learning.

Before moving on to Chapter 7, I'll end with one encouragement. If some efforts are currently in place, I hope that this chapter has affirmed those efforts or provided suggestions for how they may be refined or supplemented. If no such information gathering currently exists, I hope that this chapter has provided some compelling rationales for initiating it. There is a range of options such that there is surely an option that aligns well with a preacher's personal preference, comfort level, information needs, or the traditions within a local congregation or denomination. Some investment in gathering information about preaching and learning—starting somewhere—will be a worthwhile initiative.

CHAPTER 7

The Critical Friend

THE PREVIOUS CHAPTER EMPHASIZED the importance of and methods for gathering two kinds of feedback: 1) information about what listeners learn from a sermon and 2) formative information for the preacher's use to consider changes that can improve listeners' learning. This chapter focuses exclusively on the latter goal of sermon improvement and presents a process involving what I call the *critical friend*. First, I'll define that concept; then I'll describe a process for using a critical friend to gain insight into sermon development, delivery, and impact on listeners.

WHAT IS A CRITICAL FRIEND?

I suppose we could all define a *friend*. A friend is more than just an acquaintance. It is someone you can count on. Someone you trust. Someone who is on your side. Someone in whom you can confide without concern that the friend will betray your confidence. Someone who has your back, regardless of the circumstances you face.

Combined with the adjective, *critical*, the term *critical friend* connotes a bit more. In many situations, "critical" carries a connotation of negativity, nit-picking, or nay saying. Not in this case. An alternative usage of the term "critical" connotes careful analysis, judgment or evaluation of the merits of something as in "the author's first novel received much critical acclaim." As used in this chapter, the "critical" modifier describes a friend who is candid but supportive, thoughtful but open, sensitive but analytic. The critical friend provides feedback that is oriented toward development, improvement, and encouragement. Defined this way, who *wouldn't* want a critical

The Critical Friend

friend? We all could use a critical friend, but preachers have a special need for such a relationship.

Preachers need a critical friend for the realm of creating and delivering sermons. I will describe the specific steps in the critical friend process shortly, but first I'll pose the rhetorical question: Wouldn't it be great to have a trusted colleague who could provide confidential, supportive, encouraging, formative input on a sermon? Someone who was "on the inside" in terms of what the preacher was trying to accomplish and could give ideas, reactions for the plan to do so? Someone who, after listening to a sermon, could help the preacher reflect on what seemed to really work well and might have been done differently.

In addition to the characteristics of a critical friend listed earlier, there is an additional characteristic that is valuable—no, necessary—in the context of preparing and delivering sermons; namely, the avoidance of a power relationship. The most beneficial critical friend relationships are ones in which the critical friend is not within the preacher's sphere of authority or responsibility. An optimal candidate for a critical friend is thus *not* the chair of the elder board, a deacon, a long-time member in good standing, a bishop, an overseer, one's spouse or relative, or any other person for which there would be the potential—in perception or in reality—for a power relationship to be in play. In short, a potential critical friend should not be someone in any evaluative, supervisory, or subordinate role with respect to the preacher.

Seasoned preachers are surely already aware of these, but I'll pose some hypothetical situations that illustrate perceptions of a power relationship that would compromise the ability of a person to serve as a critical friend:

- The chair of the elder board whose family has been church members for generations worries that, if she gives candid feedback to the pastor, she may not be supported for another term.
- A new member of a church is concerned that, if the pastor takes her input the wrong way, the pastor may not visit her dying mother in the hospital but send a lay minister in his stead.
- A priest in one parish has second thoughts about asking a priest from another local parish or the diocesan bishop to serve as a critical friend because exposing his weaknesses in delivering homilies might

diminish his chances for advancement or movement when a sought-after position opens up.

I don't believe that any humble pastor would respond in the ways above. What I do believe is that the potential candidates for a preacher's critical friend described in the preceding scenarios might logically *think* those things and be less likely to provide honest, supportive, critical feedback. Yet it's exactly that kind of input that would be the most constructive and helpful. It's that kind of feedback that has the greatest potential to motivate changes that can make the difference between a message that is *heard* and one that is *learned*—a sermon that prompts real, lasting changes in listeners' lives. It takes courage and trust for someone to give, and a preacher to receive, input along the lines of the following in which trusted friend says to the preacher:

- "I think some kind of a transition between the two main portions of that sermon seems missing. If you could include a transition, I think it would help listeners better grasp the connection between them."
- "Any other time, I think people really appreciate the way you inject a bit of levity to break up some serious points you make. However, I'd really advise against that bit of humor you're thinking of using in your Good Friday sermon. I think it has the potential to be received by a number of people in the congregation as inappropriate or disrespectful of a solemn, holy day."
- "That one example is a good one, but my sense is that it might only seem relevant to the younger adults in the congregation. Have you thought about including another example or two that would connect with other groups of folks?"
- "I'm guessing you know this, but you have a habit of tugging at your left earlobe frequently as you are preaching. I get the impression that a lot of folks find that to be really distracting for them and distracts them from focusing on the sermon." (Recall from Chapter 1 my habit of saying "um" so frequently.)
- "I know what you want to get across as the main idea in that sermon, but it just seems like the main idea is languishing in the background and kind of gets lost. Are there some ways that you could reorganize to bring the main idea front and center?"

The Critical Friend

The critical friend who could provide the preacher with supportive, non-threatening questions and suggestions along these lines would be a great aid not only to the preacher in preparing, delivering, and self-assessing a sermon, but would help listeners by facilitating greater understanding, recall, and application of the sermon content. Ultimately, it would foster greater impact on their lives. A critical friend can be an important part of that if the right environment is created and an appropriate feedback process followed. In the next section, I'll describe how to create the right environment and I'll focus in detail on the steps in the process.

I want to first note that I write with some experience about the critical friend process. In the preface to this book, I mentioned an early career mentor for me, Professor Steve Yelon. I was enrolled in a PhD program at Michigan State University where I had been offered a fellowship to pursue a doctorate in the educational psychology department. As a condition (and benefit, I came to see) of that award, I would be teaching an introductory level Educational Psychology course. In fact, I'd be teaching many of them—about two sections each semester for three years. However—and this was the catch—I was required to arrive on campus early in the summer before my first semester and to participate in an orientation to teaching at the university level.

"No sweat," I thought. My undergraduate degree was in teaching, and I'd already taught in an elementary school for five years, so I'd learned a lot about teaching under challenging conditions. Teaching undergraduate courses would be easy; nothing could be tougher than working with children who literally don't know which way is right and which is left, helping a student who was throwing up during the spelling lesson, mediating playground fights, ensuring that the 2nd grader whose parents were vegetarians got the right soy dog at the end-of-year picnic.

I was wrong. I had not yet met Professor Yelon.

He didn't use the term *critical friend* at the time, but he laid the foundation. In the weeks before the opening of my first fall semester as a university instructor, he led an intensive orientation in which he taught and modeled what it meant to be a critical friend. In various ways, he first made us feel certain of several things: He was on our side. He wanted nothing more than for us to be successful. Any input he would give us would be honest, compassionate correction, enthusiastic encouragement. He was going to be there for us, getting us ready to develop and deliver the course content. His ultimate aim was to lead us through some instructional design principles and mentor us as teachers in a way that would help our students learn and help them be successful.

That summer session was intensive but rewarding. The process Professor Yelon led us through was collegial and challenging. In the first few meetings of our seminar group, he helped us think through what we were planning to teach. He helped us develop plans for our instruction. He gave suggestions for us to consider about how to tweak those lessons. As a next step, he watched us teach mini lessons one-on-one. That might have been intimidating—presenting a lesson to an expert mentor—but we knew he only wanted us to be the most effective teachers we could be, which was a goal he knew we had in common. Eventually, we videotaped our first few, real, class meetings of the fall semester when we were on our own as instructors for our courses. Shortly after a class session, he would watch the video of a class session with us individually, and together we'd talk about what we saw and heard. He helped us to analyze the instructional decisions that we made, the options we might have considered. and we discussed our rationales for choosing one path or another.

Did I mention his feedback was challenging? For example, in some of the courses I had taken several years earlier as an undergraduate preparing to be an elementary school teacher, I was (mis)informed about giving feedback to students. I recall one instructor talking to us about classroom management—a difficult task for first year teachers at any grade level. The teacher showed us a video of a student misbehaving in class and asked for our opinions about how we might handle the situation. We gave various suggestions, but as it turned out there was only one correct answer being pushed in the 1970s: positive reinforcement. We weren't supposed to correct a student for his or her misbehavior. We weren't supposed to suggest that the student had done anything wrong. We were supposed to focus on the positive aspects of something the student had done. I recall distinctly the instructor telling us there was really only one correct reaction in all such situations. It was the mantra of the day: "Praise him. Just praise him. Take every opportunity to praise him." It felt like I was in a worship service.

Fast forwarding to the college teaching orientation I received years later with Professor Yelon, it was clear he didn't subscribe to that philosophy. He definitely commended us on strategic choices we made that would help our students learn. But he also recognized that the best approach to helping us improve was to address choices that were not likely to be helpful. Harmful decisions—and thankfully I made only a few of those—were pointed out in a clear, firm way, but also done in the same supportive way as he pointed out helpful decisions.

Later in my career, I adapted what my mentor had taught me about being a critical friend in other contexts. I served many times as a colleague observer of other faculty members' teaching. I mentored junior faculty interested in improving their teaching. I also applied the concept of a critical friend in preparing some of the books I've written. As the editor of a volume, I might work with a dozen or more authors of individual chapters. At the start of the process, I helped each author identify a critical friend for his or her chapter. These volunteers were scholars who were familiar with the topic of the chapter they would be reviewing, and they agreed to provide feedback to the chapter author on their initial draft of the chapter. I often didn't see the feedback; it was between the chapter author and the critical friend. Technically, chapter authors could ignore the feedback provided by the critical friend, but they uniformly reported that the critical friend's feedback—including both commendations and suggestions for revisions—was immensely helpful in producing a final chapter draft that was clearly better for engaging in the critical friend process.

THE CRITICAL FRIEND ENVIRONMENT AND PROCESS

How might the critical friend process be applied to preaching? Seven elements characterize an effective critical friend process. Each of the elements is described in the following sections and summarized in Table 7-1.

Identifying Potential Candidates for a Critical Friend

The choice of a critical friend is one of the most important steps in the process. Who might be a good critical friend? Let's first review who it *shouldn't* be. Earlier I listed various people who would not be a good choice: the chair of the elder board, a deacon, a long-time member of the congregation, a bishop, one's spouse, and so on. I suggested that any existing relationship where a power dynamic might be in play should be avoided. Equally important, however, is the existence of a trust relationship—or the foundation for and willingness to build one. The effectiveness of the critical friend relationship depends on both parties entering into it with goodwill and openness. The preacher must be assured that the critical friend is exclusively committed to being helpful and that he or she will hold all conversations in confidence. The critical friend must be sensitive and assured that any input will be accepted as constructive feedback for consideration.

Table 7-1
Elements of the Critical Friend Process

Element	Description
1	Identify Potential Candidates for a Critical Friend
2	Selection of a Critical Friend and Setting Expectations
3	Becoming Familiar with the Preaching Context
4	The Pre-meeting
4a	Review of observation contexts
4b	Review of intended sermon goals
5	The Sermon Observation
6	Critical Analysis & Reflection
7	The Post-meeting

Thus, there is a limited universe from which to identify a potential critical friend. One option might be a colleague with which a preacher has made a connection through a local interfaith organization or quarterly pastors' lunch. Another preacher from within the preacher's denomination but outside of the local organizational structure is another option. A classmate from seminary or subsequent conference, retreat, or similar experience can be a good option.[1]

In addition to the general characteristics of a critical friend listed above, other specific characteristics should be considered. He or she should have adequate time to devote to the process. The critical friend should be a good listener. He or she should be willing to learn about and sensitive to relevant local church history, demographics and diversity within the preacher's congregation. Ideally, some background in learning theory or mentoring in instructional settings would be helpful. The critical friend should be skilled in providing formative feedback in ways that are candid and specific, but constructive and encouraging. If a potential critical friend has no other qualifications than those listed in the previous section, a wise

---

[1]. To extend the potential support that this book might be for preachers, the companion website for this book, www.sermonscience.com lists individuals with relevant background and experience to serve as a critical friend.

activity to discern if there is the potential for a preacher/critical friend relationship would simply be for both parties to read this chapter, discuss its contents, and determine if both could be on the same page going forward.

Selection of a Critical Friend and Setting Expectations

The primary result of the second element in the critical friend process is the selection of the person to serve in that role and the agreement among both individuals to move forward (or not) with the next steps in the critical friend process. Any agreement need not be a formal document, although having a written record of expectations, agreements, and responsibilities can be helpful. As a component of the agreement, the expectations of each party should be made explicit and discussed. The expectations should be realistic and mutually agreed upon. They should include practical specifications such as start date, sermon(s) to be observed, meeting dates and modalities, assurance concerning confidentiality, time to be allocated to the process, limits and procedures for reimbursement of expenses (if any), and conclusion dates for the process. At this point, the preacher may wish to provide advance readings, printed or electronic copies of previous sermons in a series, or other materials that deemed desirable for the critical friend to review. Similarly, the critical friend might provide notes or other information (possibly drawn from this chapter) that would provide additional information to the preacher regarding the critical friend process. If desired by both parties, an on-going or reciprocal relationship might be discussed.

Becoming Familiar with the Preaching Context

Once the critical friend relationship has been affirmed, it is important for the critical friend to become familiar with what will be observed and with the contextual features of that observation. This element is primarily the responsibility of the critical friend. He or she must become familiar with the preacher's style, with the preacher's personality as it comes through in preaching, with relevant demographic characteristics of the congregation (e.g., age, general educational level, language, ethnicity, worship traditions), and with the sensibilities of the congregation as those are evident in their reactions to the preacher's sermons. This could be accomplished by the critical friend actually attending one or more sermons and, as unobtrusively as possible, listening, taking notes, and observing the ways in which the preacher and congregation interact. Although best accomplished in person, in the digital age this need not require physical attendance. It can often be easily facilitated by attending a service remotely, connecting via livestream broadcast of a sermon, or viewing/listening to a sermon via podcast or selections from a sermon archive. The critical friend's observations and notes from this element form the foundation of the next element.

The Pre-Meeting

After the critical friend has achieved some confidence and comfort with the context that characterizes the sermon that will be observed, a meeting should occur between the critical friend and the preacher in which two essential purposes are addressed. I refer to this meeting as a "Pre-Meeting" to connote that it precedes the critical friend's observation of one or more future sermons, and to distinguish it from a second meeting that occurs following the next sermon observation.

First, the logistics of the Pre-Meeting are important. A single Pre-Meeting is usually sufficient, and setting aside a single two-hour block of time is typically enough to accomplish the goals of the Pre-Meeting. Ideally, the Pre-Meeting would be a face-to-face, in-person meeting (or perhaps more than one such meeting if deemed appropriate). Although not ideal, a Zoom or other virtual format can also work. Many venues are possible—the preacher's go-to coffee shop that provides a quiet and disturbance-free place to read, counsel, or study, a local park, the public library. However, in most cases, the optimal meeting location is the preacher's study, office, a church conference room or other location familiar to the preacher, where he or should has ready access to his or her notes, library, or other resources that might be useful to access during the meeting. Of primary importance is that the location provides a venue that is conducive to confidential conversations. It should be a place that is comfortable and should be scheduled so that the time can be focused and uninterrupted.

The first main purpose of the Pre-Meeting is to provide time for critical friend and the preacher to assess understandings of both parties related to any advance readings; to answer questions or concerns that have arisen; and to discuss the critical friend's information and conclusions related to the congregation and context based on his or her observations gleaned in Step 3. Because of the limited amount of time that a critical friend will have to attend or review prior sermons, the information and conclusions made will necessarily be tentative—and perhaps inaccurate in some cases—so a meeting to confirm, correct, or revise any perceptions is essential. The critical friend should describe what was observed. Then, her or she should ask questions or seek clarifications from the preacher as needed regarding, for example (but not limited to), questions that came to mind about:

- congregational characteristics,
- the sermon context,
- technologies utilized,
- aspects of the preacher's style,
- and perceived reactions of the congregation to various aspects of the sermon.

At the Pre-Meeting meeting, the preacher can confirm the conclusions, add historical background or other relevant information that may have been unavailable or missed, and provide additional context that will aid the critical friend in gaining a better understanding of the relationship between the preacher and the congregation.

The kinds of discussion that might occur at the Pre-Meeting could be prompted by the critical friend asking questions such as:

> "I thought there was a fairly casual format in the sermons I observed. You seemed comfortable moving around the front of the sanctuary; I saw several listeners sipping coffee; people seemed to feel free to make comments to each other during the sermon, but the comments appeared to be relevant to the sermon and not just side conversations. Are these things characteristic of the typical sermon environment? Is the level of casualness something that you have tried to cultivate? Is it something you and the congregants are comfortable with? Are you contemplating any changes to this format?
>
> "In the sermons I listened to, when you cited a Scripture, your quotations were exclusively from the King James Version of the Bible. Is that an expectation or tradition within your congregation?"
>
> "I noticed that you often included a humorous story, brief quip, or anecdote in each sermon. It looked like your congregation really appreciates that. Is that part of your style, only an occasional occurrence, or something that you have learned that is important to include regularly?"
>
> "The two sermons I listened to seemed to be part of a series of sermons, with maybe eight sermons overall in the series. Are your

sermons typically series-based; are they most often stand-alone sermons, or do you alternate between those?"

In summary, the first purpose of the Pre-Meeting element is for the critical friend to acquire a better understanding of the preaching context, to gain relevant background on the characteristics of the congregation, to verify assumptions, and to acquire a framework for the second purpose.

Once the critical friend and the preacher have common understandings and as complete a picture as possible given the constraints, the Pre-Meeting then turns to its second primary purpose: description of the future sermon to be observed. At least at the beginning of a critical friend relationship, it is preferable to focus on one, specific, upcoming sermon.[2] In this portion of the Pre-Meeting conversation, the preacher lays out for the critical friend what he or she will be attempting to accomplish in an upcoming sermon that will be the focal event of the process. The exact date of the critical friend's observation of that sermon will be arranged at this time, as will the date for a Post-Meeting that occurs following the actual sermon observation and a time of reflection and analysis by the critical friend.

Of greatest importance during the Pre-Meeting are that the preacher describes for the critical friend:

- the topic and goals for that sermon
- the precursor sermons that have provided the background for the sermon and, if relevant, where the future sermon fits into a sermon series
- the main idea(s) that will be the focus of the sermon
- the planned organizational structure of the sermon and the relationship of the sermon plan for accomplishing its goals
- the specific aspects of sermon development or delivery about which the preacher would like formative feedback.
- any unique or novel strategies that the preacher intends to incorporate, and
- any anticipated congregational reactions or responses to the sermon.

If nothing else, there is one outcome of the Pre-Meeting that must be achieved: the preacher and critical friend must arrive at a common

2. It is suggested to focus on a single sermon (or, at most two contiguous sermons) as a starting point for the critical friend process. Additional sermon observations could be added subsequently, if both parties mutually agree that continuing the critical friend relationship would be desirable.

understanding of the preacher's purpose for the sermon. To further clarify this point, the common understanding must be *the understanding that the preacher has in mind*. It is that understanding that is discussed and communicated in the Pre-Meeting and which must be fully grasped by the critical friend. Ideally, the preacher's goals for the sermon should be formalized and captured in writing, reviewed, discussed, refined, and ultimately confirmed by the preacher as faithfully capturing the intention.

An important additional note in terms of gaining understanding of the sermon goals is this: the goals of the sermon to be observed are *not* the goals that the critical friend has in mind or influenced by his or her notions of what might be desirable. The critical friend relationship exists solely in service to the preacher's aims. The preacher has far greater insights into the spiritual needs of the congregation, local church history and traditions, topics that have been covered in previous sermons, Sunday school meetings, weekday services, and so on. In short, the key outcome of the Pre-Meeting should result in the sermon observation being sharply and exclusively focused on what the preacher intends for the sermon to accomplish.

Finally, the critical friend and the preacher should review and tailor the observational checklist that will be used to focus the observation. A sample observation checklist is provided as Table 7-2, and additional information on the checklist and its use is provided in the following section.

The Sermon Observation

With a good grasp of what the preacher intends to accomplish in a sermon and the plan for doing so, the next step in the process is for the critical friend to attend and listen to the sermon on the agreed upon date. Again, ideally, this observation would be done in person, allowing the critical friend to view the entire environment and to make informal observations of the context, listener reactions, and other features that are not well captured in an online mode of presentation. The critical friend should arrive early enough to be seated in a location that will allow him or her to view projected materials (if any) and to hear the sermon clearly.

The chosen location should also be discrete, in that the critical friend will want to make occasional notes in a way that does not distract other listeners or the preacher. Any notes might be taken on paper (perhaps using the framework shown in Table 7-2) or, where congruent with congregational norms, on a tablet, laptop, or other personal device. In many contexts, a recording of a sermon is routinely captured; if not—and if it is agreeable to the preacher and can be done in a way that is not disruptive—a recording of the sermon can be a valuable adjunct to the critical friend's notes. In sum, in the ideal situation, as any visitor might do, the critical friend would simply blend unobtrusively into the congregation, participate in the service, and not attract undue attention in the course of conducting the sermon observation.

An effective critical friend will attend to several aspects of the sermon. Table 7-2 provides a sample checklist of sermon elements on which the preacher may want the critical friend to focus. The checklist contains five columns. The first three columns are for the observer to record whether something was Observed (O), Not Observed (N), or is Not Applicable (NA). The fourth column lists potential Sermon Aspects that might be the focus of the observation. As described previously, the specific Sermon Aspects to be observed should be agreed upon by the preacher and critical friend in advance of the observation as a concluding activity of the Pre-Meeting. Checklist entries can be added at that time depending on the areas on which the preacher wants input or depending on what is most relevant to the specific sermon topic, style, or local church norms. Aspects listed in Table 7-2 that are deemed not relevant for an observation can be deleted or ignored. Conversely, a preacher may have specific aspects of a sermon that he or she would want to be a focus of the observation. Blank rows at the bottom of the Sermon Aspects column allow for inclusion of those additional aspects.

A fifth column is labeled "Notes" and provides a place for the critical friend to elaborate on anything observed. The little amount of space provided in the Notes column is purposeful. The essential activity of the critical friend observing a sermon is to be fully engaged in listening to the sermon. Only the most minimal notations necessary to jog his or her memory for subsequent discussion should be made. Minimal notetaking will, in some contexts, be necessary to avoid disruption or attracting undue attention. To the extent that it is within the technology norms of the congregation, a video recording of the sermon should be made available to the critical friend so that all important aspects need not be written as comments, enabling the critical friend to focus primarily on the sermon during its delivery. The sermon presentation can then be re-viewed as needed at any time after the observation.

Table 7-2
Sample Critical Friend Sermon Observation Checklist[3]

O	N	NA	Sermon Aspects	Notes/Suggestions
☐	☐	☐	The main idea was clearly presented early in the sermon.	
☐	☐	☐	Sermon topic did not require listener background knowledge (or sufficient background or review was provided during sermon to facilitate listener understanding).	
☐	☐	☐	Other key points in the sermon supported the main idea.	
☐	☐	☐	Sermon organization and delivery appeared to engage listeners.	
☐	☐	☐	Transitions between major portions of the sermon were clear and effective.	
☐	☐	☐	Examples were provided to illustrate key points.	
☐	☐	☐	Examples used were relevant, sensitive to listener characteristics, and effective in supporting key ideas.	
☐	☐	☐	Technology used (if any) supported sermon goals.	
☐	☐	☐	Humor used (if any) was relevant and supported sermon goals.	
☐	☐	☐	Sermon pacing was appropriate.	
☐	☐	☐	Sermon length was appropriate/maintained listener engagement.	
☐	☐	☐	Language used was appropriate to listener characteristics.	
☐	☐	☐	Novel terminology used or unfamiliar concepts referenced in the sermon were defined and illustrated.	
☐	☐	☐	Listener reactions appeared to reflect understanding of sermon content.	
☐	☐	☐		
☐	☐	☐		
☐	☐	☐		

3. The example shown is available for free download in the Resources section of www.SermonScience.com

A final caveat regarding the observation is important: Readers may notice that the checklist of sermon elements focuses exclusively on the teaching aspects of the sermon—organization, structure, examples, transitions, presentation, and so on. Sermon content is not only unrepresented in the checklist but is off limits in the critical friend process. That is, the critical friend relationship exists solely to support the preacher toward the goal of helping listeners learn from the sermon. It is not a mechanism for raising potential disagreements about theological issues, Scriptural interpretations, or denominational doctrines.

Critical Analysis and Reflection

Having completed the sermon observation, the critical friend then engages in a time of reflection on what was observed in preparation for the Post-Meeting. There are three sources of information that provide the foundation necessary for a critical analysis of the sermon event:

1) *The preacher's intended goals.* This is the primary benchmark against which the critical friend will form eventual reactions and suggestions. The primary question that the critical friend will aid the preacher in answering is: "To what extent did the goals I had for my sermon appear to be accomplished?" Notes from the Pre-Meeting—primarily the finalized statements about the preacher's sermon goals—as well as any other notes taken by the critical friend during that meeting will be helpful sources of information to focus the analysis.

2) *A recording of the sermon.* As mentioned previously, if available, an audio or video recording of the sermon provides a helpful source of information, particularly as a resource for the critical friend regarding aspects of the sermon that may not have been observed or perceived incorrectly. When a person is engaged in writing down a note, an important point can be missed. A recording may be useful to clarify portions of a sermon about which the critical friend is concerned that he or she may not have heard or heard incorrectly.

3) *The critical friend's observation notes.* The notes taken during the observation will aid the critical friend to recall his or her reactions in the moment, how aspects of the sermon appeared to be received by listeners, and details from the sermon that seemed especially relevant to helping or hindering what the preacher was intending to accomplish.

In brief, the outcome of this period of reflection and analysis is a set of notes that examine the correspondence between two states: what the preacher had outlined as goals for the sermon and the extent to which those goals appeared to be achieved. The translational aspects between these two states comprise the formative feedback that will be shared with the preacher and form the basis for the conversation that takes place in the final, Post-Meeting, step of the process.

Here, *translational aspects* refer to the mechanisms that account for the correspondence between the two states. For example, if the preacher had identified Goal X as important and that goal appeared to have been accomplished, the critical friend can provide feedback that helps bring into focus the aspects of the sermon organization or delivery that aided in the success of accomplishing Goal X. Conversely, the critical friend may have observed that another of the preacher's goals, Goal Z, did not appear to be accomplished to the same degree. In that case, a skilled critical friend can provide formative feedback that identifies potential barriers that hindered accomplishing the goal, or suggestions for other strategies that may be more effective.

The Post-Meeting

The Post-Meeting is the culmination of the critical friend process. It is both a time of debriefing and supportive conversation. It is the occasion at which formative feedback is provided by the critical friend, and an opportunity for thoughtful, candid consideration regarding the extent to which the sermon goals appeared to have been accomplished, what appeared to help listeners to learn from the sermon as presented, and a time of posing and evaluating suggestions that might increase clarity, effectiveness, listener engagement and learning.

As with the Pre-Meeting, logistics should be considered. There are certainly exigencies that might arise that would necessitate a virtual meeting, but in nearly all cases, an in-person meeting is preferable. A single Post-Meeting may suffice, although more than one meeting might be needed depending on the depth of discussions and the number of sermon aspects that the preacher is interested in pursuing. At minimum, an effective Post-Meeting requires between two and three hours, allowing for breaks as appropriate. If additional time is desired, it is optimal to schedule the Post-Meetings as two-hour blocks on days that are reasonably close in time so that the flow of the conversations is maintained. Like the Pre-Meeting, the preacher is best qualified to identify a location of choice for the Post-Meeting. The Post-Meeting could occur in the same place as the Pre-Meeting to the extent that ready access to resources (e.g., sermon notes on the preacher's desktop computer, books or other references relevant to the sermon, and so on) would be helpful. Again—and perhaps even more so for the Post-Meeting—the key consideration is that the location provides a venue that is conducive to confidential conversations and provides a comfortable, uninterrupted environment where focused conversations can take place.

Prior to the Post-Meeting, and during the same period as the critical friend is engaging in the critical analysis and reflection element, it is helpful (though not necessary) for the preacher to engage in a similar time of reflection about the sermon. Table 7-3 shows parallel questions that the critical friend and preacher could be considering in this time. As with other examples of surveys and checklists provided in this book, additional rows are provided at the bottom of Table 7-3 to highlight that the list of questions should be expanded to align to the specific areas on which a preacher wants to focus.

There are three ways that the questions in Table 7-3 can be used. The table can be used as an effective way to structure the Post-Meeting. The critical friend and preacher can simply use the questions to frame conversations in which they share and compare answers and reflections on the topics embodied by the questions. Alternatively, it is not necessary for the preacher to review and consider the questions in advance. It is perfectly acceptable and equally beneficial if the Post-Meeting is organized around the last two columns of the table. The critical friend can simply raise the questions listed in the "Critical Friend" column for discussion. In the course of the discussion, a skilled critical friend engages not merely in conversation about the sermon, but provides thoughtful insights based on the observations and suggestions—formative feedback—for the preacher's consideration.

Table 7-3
Possible Reflection Questions that Can Provide Structure for the Post-Meeting[4]

Preacher	Critical Friend	Follow Up
In a sentence or two, what was I trying to accomplish in this sermon?	Overall, how would you summarize what the sermon was trying to accomplish?	
What was my main point (or points) of the sermon?	What did it seem was the main point (or points) of the sermon? Did that change at all from what you had originally planned?	
Overall, how did the sermon seem to go?	Overall, how do you think the sermon seemed to go?	
How did it seem the listeners were engaged in the sermon?	How did it seem to you that listeners were engaged in the sermon?	✓
Which examples seemed to be helpful, not as helpful?	Which examples do you think were most helpful to your listeners; which seemed least helpful?	✓
What aspects of technologies used (if any) were helpful, may need improvement?	What aspects of technologies used (if any) seemed helpful; which do you think may need improvement?	✓
Did listeners seem to grasp the main point(s)/ what I was trying to accomplish?	Do you think your listeners seemed to grasp the main point(s)/ the sermon was trying to accomplish?	
What key decision points in sermon development might I revisit?	What key decisions in sermon development do you think might have been consequential in terms of listener learning/ engagement?	
If I tried any new ideas or techniques in terms of delivery style, organization, or ways of communicating, how did they appear to work? Which might I continue to incorporate, revise, or omit in the future?	If any new ideas or techniques in terms of delivery style, organization, or ways of communicating, were incorporated, how did they appear to work? Which are you thinking you might continue incorporate, revise, or omit in the future?	✓
What specific things appeared to go well?	What specific things appeared to go well?	
What specific things didn't seem to go very well? Why?	What specific things didn't seem to go very well? Why?	
What would I consider doing differently in terms of organization, delivery, examples, etc.?	What are you considering doing differently in terms of organization, delivery, examples, etc.?	

4. The example shown is available for free download in the Resources section of www.SermonScience.com

The third way in which the framework shown in Table 7-3 can be used is related to the third column with the heading "Follow Up." As can be seen in the table, there are check marks in four of the rows. These indicate questions that, based on the sermon observation, notes, and (if relevant) review of an audio or video of the sermon, the critical friend identifies as areas of focus for the Post-Meeting discussion. The following provide hypothetical examples of such follow up related to the first two checked categories in the Reflection Questions Checklist.

Regarding the question on listener engagement, the critical friend may have observed that listeners were engaged for the first half of a sermon but appeared to become less interested as the sermon progressed. It would seem important to understand this occurrence. Did the preacher sense the same phenomenon? Has that happened for previous sermons? If so, do there seem to be commonalities in those situations? Was timing misjudged? Both the preacher and the critical friend might posit ideas as to why such a shift in attention may have taken place. A critical friend might ask: "What changes in the sermon organization, delivery, or other strategies might be considered to see if they affect that shift?" A skilled critical friend can offer suggestions about such changes.

To elaborate on how the checklist might be used to structure a Post-Meeting discussion, let us consider the second checkmark in the row dealing with examples. The critical friend might begin the conversation directly with an observation:

> *"I noticed that every example used to illustrate a point in the sermon was one taken from experiences in your family: one was from your family vacation last summer; three were about your wife, Kimberly; the other two involved experiences with your children. Clearly, family is important to you and has provided you with a lot of important insights. I wonder, however, if it might be helpful to broaden the context of the illustrations used. For example, I noticed what seemed to be quite a few single attendees and even what appeared to be a few homeless persons. Regardless, I suspect that there are often many people in any congregation who didn't have a supportive home life growing up, who come from single-parent homes, and maybe some who still have anger or no connection with one or more of their parents. In those cases, they aren't likely to have the frame of reference that would make some examples as helpful as they might be. I'm NOT saying to stop using family examples—they can be great—I'm just thinking that varying the contexts might help listeners. Perhaps drawing on diverse family structures, or even going beyond family*

context and mixing in workday contexts, social contexts, or other situations so that the point has a chance to connect with more of the listeners might be a good idea. What do you think? I mean, you know the people in your congregation best and it looks like there are a lot of families, but are there other contexts represented that you think could be drawn in?"

CONCLUSION

Those who develop and deliver sermons do not often have the opportunity to get candid, constructive feedback about their sermons from a trusted, thoughtful, and supportive colleague. The critical friend process is a variation of a mentoring model in the field of teaching and learning, and it incorporates several elements that have been shown to be effective in improving performance. Identifying and enlisting a critical friend can provide a powerful avenue for a preacher to obtain helpful, formative feedback on sermon development and delivery. Sermon development and delivery are merely intermediate goals, however. The ultimate aim of establishing and engaging in a critical friend relationship is downstream, affecting the learning and application of sermon content that prompts spiritual growth and changed lives, not only on the part of listeners, but also those they encounter in their lives.

CHAPTER 8

Dear Pastor

A COMPELLING NARRATIVE ABOUT giving sermons is contained in a book by Marvin McMickle:

> "During my first pastorate . . . one of the deacons would ask me the same question every Sunday morning . . . 'Reverend, is there any word from the Lord?'. . . The voice that people want to hear is not really the voice of the preacher. The voice that people really need to hear is not that of the preacher. The message the people have assembled to receive is not whatever wit or wisdom may be on our mind any given Sunday."[1]

The purpose of the preceding chapters in this book was to apply some of what learning scientists have discovered related to helping listeners grasp, retain, and use to the context of developing and delivering sermons. Hopefully, the content of those chapters has provided some helpful principles to consider when starting from scratch or when tweaking a sermon so that it accomplishes the goal of aiding listeners to learn, recall, and apply the important truths that a preacher has attempted to convey.

This chapter has a different purpose. I'll be shifting focus away from presenting and illustrating the application of scientific principles of learning and toward the sentiment in the title of this chapter: "Dear Pastor." In this concluding chapter, I wanted to return to the second of the four critical elements of preaching identified by Thomas Long: the preacher.[2] In fact, I will sharpen that focus even further to dwell on a single word, *dear*.

---

1. McMickle, cited in Long, *The Witness of Preaching*, p. 58.
2. Long, *The Witness of Preaching*, 16.

I think that those who develop and deliver sermons are dear indeed. I don't know how often that sentiment is communicated to those who preach. As I have observed, congregants filing out of church on Sunday sometimes comment along the lines of, "That was a nice sermon, Pastor." Perhaps homilists receive an occasional positive text message, an affirming email, a Facebook "like," or an uplifting X (Twitter) posting conveying appreciation for the time and effort put into the development of a sermon, or for the impact that hearing the sermon had on a church member.

I don't know how often these things happen because—as I noted at the outset—I'm not a pastor. I'm also unaware of any research on the frequency and content of feedback that pastors receive related to their sermons. If such research exists, it almost certainly fails to capture the sincerity and depth of appreciation that exists in congregations for what their pastors do.

Having spent many years as a teacher, however, I can attest that, if you haven't been under deadline each week to come up with something new and important to say, it would be easy to underestimate the time and commitment it takes. In the constellation of all the other vital responsibilities of a pastor, preaching is perhaps the most logistically, psychologically, and spiritually challenging. In my experience as a teacher, time has always been one of those logistical challenges. The minutes it takes to deliver a sermon pale in comparison to the days that can be required to develop and prepare it.

Many readers can probably empathize with time as a challenge because it is often a factor in whatever we seek to accomplish that is truly worthwhile. This fact echoes what Thomas Paine said in the context of encouraging the first Americans who were fighting in the Revolutionary War: "What we obtain too cheaply, we esteem too lightly; it is dearness only that gives everything its value."[3] Valuable and effective sermons are not obtained cheaply; the cost is great, and greatly appreciated.

A second factor that adds to the challenge of presenting a sermon is likely somewhat unique to those who teach or preach; this factor is not likely to be broadly appreciated by those who have not had to prepare and deliver a sermon. Although I've taught for nearly three decades at levels ranging from elementary school to graduate school, I still have a degree of unease whenever I'm in front of a group of students, even those with whom I'm familiar. It's even worse when I'm called on to give an invited presentation to an unfamiliar audience; in those instances, I'm usually pretty much

---

3. Payne, *The American Crisis*, 1.

terrified on the inside. Part of my own unease can be traced to nagging self-questioning: Did I prepare adequately? Is the content appropriate for this audience? Are my examples clear and relevant? Are my attempts at humor actually funny? Will this presentation be received as relevant and helpful to my listeners?

The roots of this affliction have been identified by psychologists as a specialized manifestation of anxiety known by the technical term, *imposter syndrome*. Imposter syndrome was first identified by psychological researchers in the 1980s.[4] It has only recently received focused study by researchers who have catalogued links between imposter syndrome and its consequences, including psychological distress, anxiety, and depression.[5] Imposter syndrome has also recently garnered more widespread popular attention. A recent Time magazine article proclaimed: "Yes, impostor syndrome is real: here's how to deal with it."[6]

There are many variations of imposter syndrome, but the one that applies uniquely to teachers is marked by the feeling that, despite serving in the role as a pastor or preacher, you are no better than your listeners—and perhaps not even as qualified to give guidance, speak authoritatively about sermon content, or provide spiritual direction. An inner voice screams: "You're a fake. A fraud. A poser." It is *not* a healthy form of deference, like the Scriptural admonition to "be humble, thinking of others as better than yourselves."[7] Rather, it is the anxiety related to (typically inaccurate) self-assessment and questioning.

- "How can I be preaching this, when in my own life . . . ?"
- "My brothers and sisters in this congregation—who know me very well—will surely realize that I don't have all the answers on this topic."
- "I feel like such a fraud teaching about this when I also feel like I don't have as deep an understanding of it as I'd like to have."

I have taught advanced graduate courses in my own field when I was only able to get in enough preparation beforehand to be barely one step ahead of my inquisitive and able students for that week's class meeting. Throughout the class session on that topic, I *prayed* that I wouldn't be

---

4. Clance, *The Impostor Phenomenon*.
5. Sakulku1 and Alexander, "The impostor phenomenon."
6. Abrams, "Yes, Impostor Syndrome Is Real."
7. Philippians 2:3b

pressed for further examples, explanations, or connections and exposed as an imposter posing as an expert on the topic. I imagine that the anxiety I experienced in those situations may be similar to the anxiety experienced by pastors who must, each week, speak as a spiritual leader on topics that they may not feel fully prepared to address. Indeed, the pressure—if that's the right word—on those who teach in spiritual contexts has a greater degree of seriousness reflected in the familiar Biblical caution: "Not many of you should become teachers, my fellow believers, because you know that we who teach will be judged more strictly."[8]

In addition to identifying and labeling the phenomenon of imposter syndrome, psychology has also offered prescriptions for dealing with it. Mostly, those prescriptions seem superficial. They include strategies such as recognizing and rejecting negative thoughts (easier to say than to do); recording strengths and accomplishments (easy to do, but of unknown effectiveness); and getting coaching or counseling (from psychologists, of course). In fact, there is no solid evidence of the efficacy of any of the suggestions for dealing with imposter syndrome. It may well be simply an occupational hazard of leadership.

Ironically, an effective strategy for dealing with imposter syndrome is not simply gaining greater knowledge. As other writers have noted, "A mere academic understanding of the things of God is never the way to see Him and to know Him."[9] Equally ironic is that overcoming imposter syndrome is not likely to be accomplished by hubris, but by humility.

In the previous chapter, the idea of partnering with a critical friend was suggested. Doing so clearly requires a level of trust and humility that is typically heightened as a result of positive experiences with such a friend.

Another idea has less to do with the preparation and delivery of a sermon than it does with its antecedents. I suspect that there are two characteristics that all teachers—pastors, professors, preachers and so on—have in common. The first characteristic is love of their content. In the context of spiritual life, that content is Jesus, the Word. The second characteristic is deep caring about their listeners' and their listeners' spiritual growth. I think—I hope—that even on the worst days in my own teaching, those who attend my courses, lectures, or presentations sense that I am enthusiastic about the content, but more so that I care deeply that they learn. Even if I give a "bad" lecture, I hope that my listeners are impacted by whatever

8. James 3:1 (NIV)
9. Hession and Hession, *We Would See Jesus*, 41.

affection I exude regarding the content of a lesson and its importance. Translation: Even if a pastor gives a "weak" sermon, the reflected affection for and perceived personal importance of a relationship with Jesus and love of the Scriptures will have an impact on listeners. I am convinced that we who hear a sermon are more profoundly influenced by the light within the speaker than the illumination he or she sheds on any text.

It might seem unusual to conclude a book on practical considerations for improving sermons by downplaying the impact of the very considerations covered in the preceding chapters. But it is the *preacher* and the spiritual life of the person giving a sermon that matters most. This same point has been made by others in various ways. Commenting on the danger of attention to sermon technique and stylistic features over spiritual substance, John Piper has observed that:

> "No man can give the impression that he himself is clever and that Christ is mighty to save. The temptation is huge in our day among very gifted entertainment-oriented preachers. They make a trademark out of clever speech. There is, from time to time, a place for the shrewd and penetrating riposte, but as a diet, it does not magnify Christ or feed the soul."[10]

Put differently, practical suggestions such as those in this book may be helpful, but only when embedded in the more important reality of a humble relationship with our God. We are comforted that your words are grounded in that reality. We are grateful that your sermons help show us the way. There is perhaps no more powerful example of this than in the request of a small congregation of men who expressed their simple need in a story recounted in the Gospel of John. The Scriptural account describes some Greek men who, six days before Passover went to worship at the festival in Jerusalem. The men came to the apostle Phillip with a simple request: "Sir," they said, "we would like to see Jesus."[11]

In closing, I'd like to leave a letter for all pastors that begins something like this:

---

10. Piper, quoting James Denny in *Think: The Life of the Mind and the Love of God*, 183.
11. John 12:21b (NIV); this point is drawn from Hession and Hession, *We Would See Jesus*.

Dear Pastor

Dear Pastor: I hope that some of the connections we've examined between what has been discovered regarding principles that help listeners learn will be useful as you prepare and deliver sermons. I appreciate the spiritual growth in all of us that you have prompted, aided, and deepened by your sermons. Most of all, I'm grateful for your example as the faithful servant who has developed and delivered them. Thank you for helping us see Jesus.

GJC

About the Author

Gregory J. Cizek is Guy B. Phillips Distinguished Professor of Educational Measurement and Evaluation, Emeritus, at the University of North Carolina—Chapel Hill. He began his teaching career in 1979 as a second grade teacher at Living God Christian School in Traverse City, Michigan. In 1991, Dr. Cizek received his PhD in Measurement, Evaluation, and Research Design from Michigan State University, where he first became immersed in the study of learning, assessment, and design of instruction, and he began a 32 year teaching career at the University of Toledo (Ohio) and the University of North Carolina.

Dr. Cizek has authored over 300 books, chapters, articles and conference papers at state, national and international research conferences in education, primarily the American Educational Research Association (AERA) and the National Council of Measurement in Education (NCME) for which he has served in various leadership roles, including Vice President, President, and Past President. He has delivered over 100 seminars, keynote addresses and invited presentations; he is frequently interviewed for print and broadcast media on education issues.

Dr. Cizek's work has been recognized by AERA with the E. F. Lindquist Award for Outstanding Applied or Theoretical Research in the Field of Assessment (2024) and with its award for Significant Contribution to Educational Measurement and Research Methodology (Division D, 2006). In 2007, he was honored by NCME for Outstanding Dissemination of Educational Measurement Concepts.

Over his career, Dr. Cizek has mentored numerous junior faculty, serving as research advisor and peer observer of teaching.

About the Author

Additional background on the author, resources for developing and delivering sermons, and contact information for Dr. Cizek can be found at www.SermonScience.com or by contacting the author at cizek@unc.edu.

Bibliography

7 Yards: The Chris Norton Story. Directed by Jonathon Link. 2021). Dallas, TX: Fotolanthropy.
Abrams, Abigail. "Yes, Impostor Syndrome Is Real. Here's How to Deal with It." *Time,* June 20, 2018. https://time.com/5312483/how-to-deal-with-impostor-syndrome.
Andrade, Heidi, and Gregory J. Cizek. *Handbook of Formative Assessment.* Routledge, 2010.
Atkinson, Richard C., and Richard M. Schiffrin. "Human memory: A proposed system and its control processes," *Psychology of Learning and Motivation* 2 (1968) 89–195. https://doi.org/10.1016/S0079-7421(08)60422-3.
Atkinson, Robert K., Sharon J. Derry, Alexander Renkl, and Donald Wortham. "Learning from Examples: Instructional Principles from the Worked Examples Research." *Review of Educational Research* 70, no. 2 (2000) 181–214. https://doi.org/10.2307/1170661.
Ausubel, David P. "The Use of Advance Organizers in the Learning and Retention of Meaningful Verbal Material." *Journal of Educational Psychology* 51, no. 5 (1960) 267–72. https://doi.org/10.1037/h0046669.
Bates, Anthony W. *Teaching in a Digital Age: Guidelines for Designing Teaching and Learning,* 3rd ed. 2022. https://opentextbc.ca/teachinginadigitalage/.
Berk, Ronald A. *Humor as an Instructional Defibrillator: Evidence-Based Techniques in Teaching and Assessment.* New York: Taylor & Francis, 2023.
Belluck, Pam. "To Really Learn, Quit Studying and Take a Test," *New York Times,* January 20, 2011. https://www.nytimes.com/2011/01/21/science/21memory.html
Bills, Liz, Tommy Dreyfus, John Mason, Pessia Tsamir, Anne Watson, and Orit Zaslavsky. "Exemplification in Mathematics Education" in *Proceedings of the 30th Conference of the International Group for the Psychology of Mathematics Education,* edited by Jarmila Novotná, Hana Moraová, Magdelena Krátká, and Nada Stehlíková, 126–54. Charles University, Prague, 2006. https://citeseerx.ist.psu.edu/document?repid=rep1&type=pdf&doi=0b0ec09a5d666799ff25d0376126f2fd8e1006fe#page=236.
Bloom, Benjamin S., John T. Hastings, and George F. Madaus, eds. *Handbook of Formative and Summative Evaluation of Student Learning.* New York: McGraw-Hill, 1971.
Bresee, Floyd. "How to Be a Dialogical Preacher," *Ministry: International Journal for Clergy* (May 1988) 22–3. https://www.ministrymagazine.org/archive/1988/05/how-to-be-a-dialogical-preacher.
Briggs, J. R. "Eliminate Christian Jargon from Your Church: Let's Throw Out the Insider Language, *Christianity Today,* September 19, 2017. https://www.christianitytoday.

com/pastors/2017/september-web-exclusives/eliminate-christian-jargon-from-your-church.html.

Brookhart, Susan M. *How to Give Effective Feedback to Your Students, Second Edition.* Alexandria, VA: Association for Supervision and Curriculum Development, 2017.

Bruner, Robert F. "Repetition is the First Principle of All Learning," 2001. https://ssrn.com/abstract=224340

Carrell, Lori. *The Great American Sermon Survey: The Inside Scoop on What Preachers and Their Listeners Think about Sermons.* Phoenix, AZ: Mainstay Church Resources, 2000.

Cizek, Gregory J. "The Hegemony of the Narrative: Reflections on the Contours of Social Science Research." *Review of Higher Education* 19, no. 2 (1996) 227–36.

———. "The Tale Wagging the Dog: Narrative and Neo-Pragmatism in Teacher Education and Research." In *Advances in Teacher Education, Volume 5, What Counts as Knowledge in Teacher Education*? edited by James Raths and Amy McAninch, 47–68. Norwood, NJ: Ablex, 1999.

Cizek, Gregory. J., and Samantha S. (2005). *Addressing Test Anxiety in a High-Stakes Environment.* Thousand Oaks, CA: Corwin, 2005.

Cizek, Gregory J., and Slki N. Lim. "Formative Assessment: An Overview of History, Theory, and Application." In *Elsevier Encyclopedia of Education, Volume 13*, edited by Robert. J. Tierney, Fazal Rizvi, and Kadriye Ercikan, 1–9. New York: Elsevier, 2023.

Clance, Pauline R. *The impostor phenomenon: When success makes you feel like a fake.* New York: Bantam, 1985.

Colton, David, and Robert W. Covert. *Designing and Constructing Instruments for Social Research and Evaluation.* New York: John Wiley & Sons, 2015.

Cowan, Nelson. "The magical number 4 in short-term memory: A reconsideration of mental storage capacity." *Behavioral and Brain Sciences* 24, no. 1 (2001) 87–185. DOI:10.1017/S0140525X01003922

Crites, Stephen. "The Narrative Quality of Experience. *Journal of the American Academy of Religion* 39, no. 3 (1971) 291–311.

Dabney, Robert Lewis. *Sacred Rhetoric; Or, a Course of Lectures on Preaching.* Richmond, VA: Presbyterian Committee on Publication, 1870.

Davis, Robert H., Lawrence T. Alexander, and Stephen L. Yelon. *Learning Systems Design: An Approach to the Improvement of Instruction.* New York: McGraw-Hill, 1974.

Dillman, Don A., Jolene D. Smyth, and Leah M. Christian. *Internet, Phone, Mail, and Mixed-Mode Surveys: The Tailored Design Method, 4th edition.* New York: John Wiley & Sons, 2014.

Duarte, Nancy. (2008). *Slide:Ology: The Art and Science of Creating Great Presentations.* Sebastopol, CA: O'Reilly Media, 2008.

Eareckson, Joni. (1977). *Joni.* Grand Rapids, MI: Zondervan, 1977.

Fieldstadt, Elisha. "Missouri Pastor on Leave After Sexist Sermon Preaching Wives Need to Look Good for Their Husbands." NBC News, March 8, 2021. www.nbcnews.com/news/us-news/missouri-pastor-leave-after-sexist-sermon-preaching-wives-need-look-n1259998.

Gibson, Scott. M., ed. *Preaching Points: 55 Tips for Improving Your Pulpit Ministry.* Bellingham, WA: Lexham, 2016.

———. (2020). *Tall Orders* [virtual lecture]. September 2, 2020, Truett Seminary, YouTube 43:45, https://www.youtube.com/watch?v=_9KDZ5YB1Gs.

Bibliography

Goldenberg, E. Paul. What constitutes a good example? Notes prepared for mini-conference on exemplification, Oxford, UK, June 2005.

Goldstein, Jeffrey H., and Paul E. McGhee, eds. *The Psychology of Humor*. New York: Academic, 1972.

Gordon, T. David. *Why Johnny Can't Preach: The Media Have Shaped the Messengers*. Phillipsburg, NJ: P&R, 2009.

Gregory, Marshall. *Shaped by Stories: The Ethical Power of Narratives*. South Bend, IN: University of Notre Dame Press, 2009.

Guthrie, Clinton. F. (2007). Quantitative empirical studies of preaching: A review of methods and findings. *Journal of Communication & Religion* 30, no. 1 (2007) 65–117. https://doi.org/10.5840/jcr20073013.

Hattie, John, and Helen Timperley, (2007). The power of feedback. *Review of Educational Research* 77, no. 1 (2007) 81–112. https://doi.org/10.3102/003465430298487.

Hendricks, Howard. *Teaching to Change Lives: Seven Proven Ways to Make Your Teaching Come Alive*. New York: Multnomah, 2003.

Hession, Roy, and Revel Hession. *We Would See Jesus: Discovering God's Provision for You in Christ*. Fort Washington, PA: CLC, 1958.

Hockley, William E. (2008). "The picture superiority effect in associative recognition." *Memory & Cognition* 36, no. 7 (2008) 1351–59. https://doi.org/10.3758/MC.36.7.1351

Hofstede, Geert. "Culture and Organizations." *International Studies of Management and Organization* 10, no. 4 (1980) 15–41.

———. *Culture's Consequences: Comparing Values, Behaviors, Institutions, and Organizations across Nations*. Thousand Oaks, CA: Sage, 2001.

Horne, Herman Harrell. *Jesus, the Master Teacher*. New York: Association, 1920.

Jeffery, Smart. (2023). "The Power of Storytelling: How Narratives Shape our Perception of the World." *Medium*, June 13, 2023. https://medium.com/illumination/the-power-of-storytelling-how-narratives-shape-our-perception-of-the-world-302af206cebo.

Karpicke, Jeffrey D., and William R. Aue. "The Testing Effect Is Alive and Well with Complex Materials." *Educational Psychology Review* 27, no. 2 (2015: 317–26. https://doi.org/10.1007/s10648-015-9309-3.

Krueger, Richard A., and Mary Anne Casey. *Focus Groups: A Practical Guide for Applied Research, Fifth Edition*. Thousand Oaks, CA: Sage, 2014.

Long, Thomas G. *The Witness of Preaching, 3rd edition*. Louisville, KY: Westminster John Knox, 2016.

Lorensen, Marlene Ringgaard. *Dialogic Preaching: Bakhtin, Otherness, and Homiletics*. Göttingen, Germany: Vandenhoeck & Ruprecht, 2013.

Martin, Rod, and Thomas Ford. *The Psychology of Humor: An Integrative Approach*. New York: Academic, 2018.

McCaulley, Esau. *Reading While Black: African American Biblical Interpretation as an Exercise in Hope*. Downers Grove, IL: InterVarsity, 2020.

McDaniel, Mark A., Janis L. Anderson, Mary H. Derbish, and Nova Morisette. (2007). "Testing the Testing Effect in the Classroom." *European Journal of Cognitive Psychology* 19, no. 4 (2007) 494–513. https://doi.org/10.1080/09541440701326154.

McDermott, Gerald R. (2010). *The Great Theologians: A Brief Guide*. IVP Academic, 2010.

McMickle, Marvin. A. *Living Water for Thirsty Souls: Unleashing the Power of Exegetical Preaching*. King of Prussia, PA: Judson, 2001.

McKenzie, A. M. (2016). "Form Follows Function: Well-shaped Sermons for the Twenty-first Century." In *Questions Preachers Ask: Essays in Honor of Thomas G. Long*, edited

by Scott Black Johnston, Ted A. Smith, and Leonora Tubbs Tisdale, 12–25. Louisville, KY: Westminster John Knox, 2016.
Miller, Donald G. *The Way to Biblical Preaching: How to Communicate the Gospel in Depth.* Abingdon, 1957.
Miller, G. A. (1956). "The Magical Number Seven Plus or Minus Two: Some Limits on Our Capacity for Processing Information." *Psychology Review* 63, no. 2 (1956) 81–97. https://doi.org/10.1037/h0043158.
National Research Council. *"How People Learn: Brain, Mind, Experience, and School."* Washington, DC: National Academies, 2000.
National Conference of State Legislatures. *Tips for Making Effective Powerpoint Presentations.* https://www.ncsl.org/legislators-staff/legislative-staff/legislative-staff-coordinating-committee/tips-for-making-effective-powerpoint-presentations.aspx.
Packer, James Innel. *A Passion for Faithfulness.* Wheaton, IL: Crossway, 1995.
Paivio, Allan. *Imagery and Verbal Processes.* New York: Holt, Rinehart, and Winston, 1971.
———. *Mental Representations: A Dual Coding Approach.* Oxford, UK: Oxford University Press, 1986.
Pargament, Kenneth. I., and William H. Silverman. "Exploring Some Correlates of Sermon Impact on Catholic Parishioners." *Review of Religious Research* 24, no. 1 (1982) 33–9. https://doi.org/10.2307/3510980.
Payne, Thomas. *The American Crisis, No. 1,* December 19, 1776.
Peled, Irit, and Orit Zaslavsky, O. "Counter-Examples that (Only) Prove and Counter-Examples that (also) Explain." *FOCUS on Learning Problems in Mathematics* 19, no. 3 (1997) 49–61.
Perkins, Pheme. *Jesus as Teacher.* Cambridge, UK: Cambridge University Press, 1990.
Petty, Osmond S., and Jansson, L. C. "Sequencing Examples and Non-Examples to Facilitate Concept Attainment." *Journal for Research in Mathematics Education* 18, no. 2 (1987) 112–25. https://doi.org/10.2307/749246.
Pew Research Center. "The Digital Pulpit: A Nationwide Analysis of Online Sermons." December 16, 2019. www.pewforum.org/2019/12/16/the-digital-pulpit-a-nation wide-analysis-of-online-sermons/ .
Piper, John. *Think: The Life of the Mind and the Love of God.* Wheaton, IL: Crossway, 2010.
Pollard, Tim. *The Compelling Communicator: Mastering the Art and Science of Exceptional Presentation Design.* Washington, DC: Conder House, 2016.
Procee, Gerald R. "Preaching Circles." *Christian Study Library.* https://www.christianstudylibrary.org/lib/preaching-method-and-sermon-preparation-process.
Reed, H. B. "Repetition and Association in Learning." *The Journal of Genetic Psychology* [formerly *The Pedagogical Seminary*] 31, no. 2 (1924) 147–155. https://doi.org/10.1 080/08919402.1924.10532929.
Reimann, Peter, and Thomas J. Schult. Turning Examples into Cases: Acquiring Knowledge Structures for Analogical Problem-Solving. *Educational Psychologist* 31, no. 2 (1996) 123–40. https://doi.org/10.1207/s15326985ep3102_4.
Reynolds, Garr. *Presentation Zen: Simple Ideas on Presentation Design and Delivery,* 3rd Edition. Indianapolis, IN: New Riders, 2019.
Rissland, Edwina. "Example-based Reasoning." In *Informal Reasoning in Education,* edited by James F. Voss, David N. Parkins, and Judith W. Segal, 187–208. Hillsdale, NJ: Lawrence Erlbaum, 1991.
Robinson, Haddon. W. *Biblical Preaching: The Development and Delivery of Expository Messages.* Grand Rapids, MI: Baker, 1980.

Bibliography

Rock, Irvin. (1957). "The Role of Repetition in Associative Learning." *American Journal of Psychology* 70, no. 2 (1957) 186–93. https://doi.org/10.2307/1419320.

Roediger, III, Henry L., and Jeffrey D. Karpicke. "Test-Enhanced Learning: Taking Memory Tests Improves Long-Term Retention." *Psychological Science* 17, no. 3 (2006) 249–55. https://doi.org/10.1111/j.1467-9280.2006.01693.x.

Sakulku, Jaruwan, and James Alexander. (2011). "The impostor phenomenon." *International Journal of Behavioral Science* 6, no. 1 (2011) 75–97. https://doi.org/10.14456/IJBS.2011.6.

Saplakoglu, Yasmine. "What You See in This Famous Optical Illusion Could Reveal How Old You Are." *Live Science,* September 21, 2018. www.livescience.com/63645-optical-illusion-young-old-woman.html

Scharf, Greg R. *Let the Earth Hear His Voice: Strategies for Overcoming Bottlenecks in Preaching God's Word.* Phillipsburg, NJ: P&R, 2015.

Scriven, Michael. "The Methodology of Evaluation." In *Perspectives on Curriculum Evaluation,* edited by Ralph. W. Tyler, Robert. M. Gagne, and Michael Scriven, 39–83. Chicago, IL: Rand McNally, 1967.

Smithson, Janet. "Focus Groups." In *The SAGE Handbook of Social Research Methods.* Edited by Pertti Alasuutari, Julia Brannen, and Leonard Bickman, 356–71. Thousand Oaks, CA: Sage, 2008. https://doi.org/10.4135/9781446212165.n21.

Sweller, John. "Cognitive Load During Problem Solving: Effects on Learning. *Cognitive Science* 12, no. 2 (1988) 257–85. doi:10.1207/s15516709cog1202_4.

Tennyson, Robert D., and Ok-choon Park. "The Teaching of Concepts: A Review of Instructional Design Research Literature." *Review of Educational Research* 50, no. 1 (1980) 55–70. https://doi.org/10.2307/1170030.

Tennyson, Robert D., F. Ross Woolley, and Marriner David Merrill. "Exemplar and Non-Exemplar Variables which Produce Correct Concept Classification Behavior and Specified Classification Errors." *Journal of Educational Psychology* 63, no. 2 (1972) 144–52.

Vujicic, Nick. *Nothing Is Impossible* [video]. YouTube, 4:1. https://www.youtube.com/watch?v=FXf9eNY6PLg

Ward, Adrian F., Kristen Duke, Ayelet Gneezy, and Maarten W. Bos. (2017). "Brain Drain: The Mere Presence of One's Own Smartphone Reduces Cognitive Capacity." *Journal of the Association for Consumer Research* 2, no. 2 (2017) 140–54.

White, Jr., Dan. *The Act of Dialogical Preaching: The Convergence of Conversation and Proclamation in Public Space,* 2020. http://danwhitejr.com/books/dialogical-preaching

Wiggins, Grant. "Seven Keys to Effective Feedback." *Educational Leadership* 70, no. 1 (2012) 10–16.

Wilberforce, William. *Real Christianity: Contrasted with the Prevailing Religious System.* Sisters, OR: Multnomah, 1982.

———. *A Practical View of the Prevailing Religious System of Professed Christians in the Higher and Middle Classes in This Country Contrasted with Real Christianity.* Dublin, Ireland: Robert Dapper, 1797.

Woodworth, Robert Sessions and Edward L Thorndike. "The Influence of Improvement in One Mental Function upon the Efficiency of Other Functions." *Psychological Review* 8, no. 3 (1901) 247–61. https://doi.org/10.1037/h0074898.

Yelon, Stephen L. *Powerful Principles of Instruction.* White Plains, NY: Longman, 1966.

Bibliography

Yelon, Stephen L., and Grace W. Weinstein. *A Teacher's World: Psychology in the Classroom.* New York: McGraw-Hill, 1977.

Yelon, Stephen L., and Zane L. Berge. (1988). "The Secret of Instructional Design." *Performance Improvement* 27 no. 1 (1988) 11–13.

www.ingramcontent.com/pod-product-compliance
Lightning Source LLC
Chambersburg PA
CBHW062042220426
43662CB00010B/1616